The Veteran's Money Book

The Veteran's Money Book

A Step-by-Step Program to Help Military Veterans Build a
Personal Financial Action Plan and Map Their Futures

By Mechel Lashawn Glass
with Scott Scredon

CAREER
PRESS

Pompton Plains, NJ

THE VETERAN'S MONEY BOOK
EDITED BY ROGER SHEETY
TYPESET BY DIANA GHAZZAWI
Cover design by Rob Johnson
Printed in the U.S.A.

To order this title, please call toll-free 1-800-CAREER-1 (NJ and Canada: 201-848-0310) to order using VISA or MasterCard, or for further information on books from Career Press.

CAREER
PRESS

The Career Press, Inc.
220 West Parkway, Unit 12
Pompton Plains, NJ 07444
www.careerpress.com

Library of Congress Cataloging-in-Publication Data
Glass, Mechel Lashawn.
    The Veteran's money book : a step-by-step program to help military veterans build a personal financial action plan and map their futures / by Mechel Lashawn Glass with Scott Scredon.
        pages cm
    Includes index.
    ISBN 978-1-60163-312-5 -- ISBN 978-1-60163-475-7 (ebook)
        1. Finance, Personal. 2. Veterans--Finance, Personal. I. Scredon, Scott. II. Title.
    HG179.G5434 2014
    332.0240086'970973--dc23

                                                                                    2013045966

Acknowledgments

Anyone writing about our military service members and veterans must speak with them in order to understand how they can dedicate their lives to our country and ask so little in return. We are immensely grateful to the Iraq and Afghanistan Veterans of America (IAVA), which provided us access to their members, including Nick Colgin and Matt Colvin, and that reviewed portions of our book. We are especially grateful to Daniel Buffington, who served our country in Iraq and who now works at ClearPoint Credit Counseling Solutions as a manager in our Debt Management Plan group. Daniel spent several hours helping us understand how he managed his finances while serving his country in a war thousands of miles away from home.

We also owe thanks to many people at ClearPoint. At the top of the list are Michele Pearce, the chief development officer, and our former boss, Phil Baldwin, who gave us their approval to pursue this book. We are also indebted to several of our colleagues who reviewed and edited several sections of the book, including Effie Jackson, Sue Hunt, Kevin Ferguson, Mary Ellen Nicol, and Alan Stacy. Tara Alderete was invaluable for providing the worksheets at the end of most of the chapters. Most of all, we are thankful for the stories and information provided by our credit and housing counselors, such as Randy Satterfield, Kevin Weekley, and Rachelle George. Finally, we want to thank Allie Vered, who supported the book after our former credit counseling agency merged with ClearPoint in late 2013.

We are extremely grateful to our literary agent, Grace Freedson, who believed in our proposal and took a chance on a pair of first-time authors. Finally, we owe more than we can ever express to our families. Mechel's parents, Melvin and Betty Glass, are proud to have a daughter who served in the Armed Forces and have supported her as she pursued her dreams. Scott's wife, Marcia, and his two children, Christopher and Laura, urged him for years to write a book. So he finally did.

Contents

★

Preface

Why should you read *The Veteran's Money Book*?

As you begin your transition back into civilian life, you will be faced with some major decisions. Young veterans may not know where they will live or how they will pay for basic needs, such as food, clothing, and shelter. Many others are considering returning to college so that they can start a new career. Even vets who left a stable job, and were called overseas as part of the National Guard or Reserves, may be seeking to start a new phase in their lives. This is a tough transition and you can use some help.

As a U.S. Army veteran, I can identify with the struggles you face during this time of transition. I also understand the importance of managing your money. By combining my experience as a service member with my knowledge of money, I've written a book to help you develop a personal action plan to achieve your financial goals.

If you face money problems during or after leaving military service, my story will sound familiar.

After enlisting in the U.S. Army fresh out of high school back in 1989, I had the experience of a lifetime. I worked as an intelligence analyst at a U.S. Army Field Station in Sinop, Turkey, during the first Persian Gulf War, relaying time-sensitive data in the southwest Asian theater of operations to support Desert Shield and Desert Storm. Like most service members, the experience helped me mature quickly and learn much more than if I had never enlisted.

I focused on my job and serving my country, and I didn't think much about the stable paycheck or the other financial benefits.

I made good money—but ended up blowing almost all of it. I went to bazaars and shops in Sinop, Ankara, and Istanbul to buy Turkish blankets and rugs. I never had much growing up, so I bought designer clothes, a stereo, and other electronic goods—none of which I would need 10 years down the road.

I was getting hazard pay and had few expenses. At the end of four years, I had earned more than $50,000—but little was left when it was time to separate from the service.

My parents never taught me how to manage money and there was no one in the military to educate me. So when pay day came around, I spent it all. I didn't think much about the future; I only thought about getting through the day and doing my job as well as I possibly could.

When I returned home, I was in the same predicament that many of you are in today. I had no job, no real job skills that could be transferred to the civilian world, and no place to live. I had just bought a new car and had to make monthly payments, so I needed to move back in with my parents in order to make ends meet.

It didn't seem right or fair, but after leaving the military, I was starting over. I asked myself some of the questions many of you are asking: "How did I go so quickly from having a purpose in life—serving my country during a time of war—to coming home and finding that there's nothing here for me?"

That dilemma fueled some personal problems with my family. After moving back, I wasn't the 17-year-old kid who left home, but a young woman. Unfortunately, I felt like a stranger, looking into the eyes of my parents and closest friends who I felt no longer understood me. My mother and I didn't argue or scream at one another; we just didn't speak because we didn't know what to say to each other. Six weeks after moving home, she asked me to move out.

So picture my situation: I needed to find a job quickly to pay off debt that I accumulated overseas; I was homeless, so I had to find a place to live. I quickly needed to pull myself together and make an orderly transition into a new life.

Once I collected my thoughts and analyzed the situation, I developed a plan and took action. I knew that to build a future, I had to go to college, learn new skills, and begin a career. I took advantage of the GI Bill and Tuition Assistance benefits, and by 1998, I had earned my bachelor's degree in international affairs with a minor in international business.

While going to school, I also started working for IBM Corporation. I stayed there for 11 years, receiving promotions and gradually taking on additional responsibilities. I left in 2004 to start my own company, which I eventually sold. Now I'm a vice president at one of the largest nonprofit financial counseling organizations in the country. Over the past 20 years, I learned how to use my military benefits, gained work experience at one of the best companies in the world, and taught myself how the world of money works.

That's why I know that this book will be valuable for tens of thousands, possibly hundreds of thousands of Armed Forces veterans. It will help you set up your own personal financial action plan, which will serve as a foundation for money management for the rest of your life.

We all know that whatever moves are next, it will take money to make it happen. And not only earning enough money, but carefully managing it. Chances are pretty good that during your service, you received very little information on how to handle your money.

I don't mean to be critical of the Armed Forces. Every service member has one important job, and that's to defend our country. It's the military's job to give you all of the proper training to prepare you for battle. It's not unlike any other large organization; it has a purpose, and the purpose really doesn't involve teaching or providing its members or employees with information and education on how to spend, save, and invest.

Of the 2.5 million men and women who served in the U.S. military in Iraq and Afghanistan during the past decade, many are in an excellent position to reap the financial benefits of their service. Some will come home with thousands of dollars in savings—maybe tens of thousands of dollars—plus several other benefits that will allow them to attend college at no cost to start and sustain a new career.

In effect, they are at the head of the class. They have a head start on everybody else in trying to save money and build wealth for the rest of their lives.

Unfortunately, others will struggle. Many young men and women, away from home and with money to spend, likely spent most of or all of it. For others, the stress of war—fighting every day and seeing friends die—didn't give them much reason to believe that they would be around to enjoy their future. So why save?

Here's a great story which illustrates that point. Nick Colgin served as a combat medic for 15 months as a member of the U.S. Army's 82nd Airborne Division in Afghanistan. He took part in more than 700 missions, sometimes during heavy gunfire, to try and save the lives of service members who had been wounded. After going into war zones month after month, Colgin and a buddy went on leave for 15 days. Thinking that they may not make it back alive once they returned to Afghanistan, they decided to live it up. They rented a house and together spent approximately $10,000 eating, drinking, and enjoying themselves.

"I was saving lives every day, but I thought I was going to die," Colgin said, five years after his separation from military service. "After I lived through all of the dying and the gunfire, I didn't think I was going to make it. So I spent way more money than I should have. It may have showed my youth and immaturity, but it was hard to think about my financial future during that period."

Colgin was injured in April 2008, but today he's alive and well. He left military service with a few thousand dollars in savings, but also with some debt after buying a dirt bike. While his story of service for our country is extraordinary, his financial situation upon leaving military service is not. Consider these facts about the financial lives of active duty service members and veterans:

★ Financial problems begin during active duty. The 2012 National Financial Capability Study by the Financial Industry Regulatory Authority found that 41 percent of service members find it "somewhat" or "very difficult" to cover their expenses and pay their bills; 38 percent have student loan debt and 35 percent have taken out a payday loan or used another alternative form of financing at least once during the past five years.

★ A large number of veterans need financial guidance. VeteransPlus, a national financial literacy organization dedicated to veterans, has received telephone calls or other inquiries from more than 185,000 veterans about financial concerns.

★ Veterans of all ages need help to deal with credit card debt and to avoid foreclosure. ClearPoint Credit Counseling Solutions reports that most service members and veterans seeking help about these issues are in their 40s and 50s.

If you are one of those veterans in need of financial help, here's how this book is designed to help you. Each chapter is about a specific topic. In many cases, you will also read the stories of veterans who are facing financial problems, how they have received help, and how they are developing their own action plans. At the end of each chapter, I will provide you with specific tips about how you can put your action plan into place.

For example, if you want to purchase a house or make another major purchase, I'll help you develop a strategy and tactics to accomplish this goal. If you are drowning in debt, I will help you develop a plan to address this issue.

Once the action plan is in place, the book will focus on other basic financial concepts I want you to understand. Instead of giving in to the annoying television commercials about how to get a free credit score, I want you to understand exactly how credit reports and credit scores work—and where to get the right information about your credit history for free. I also want you to be able to recognize and avoid financial scams and how to protect your assets with the right kind of insurance.

I hope that you find the book informative and that it truly helps you make a change in the way you approach your financial life. Let's get started.

1

After Military Pay Goes Away, Now What?

As a chaplain for the 278th Armored Combat Regiment stationed at Forward Operating Base Bernstein, in Iraq, Major David Clark held a wide range of duties. To help avoid any international incidents, he advised his military commander about the Islamic religion and culture. He also served as a counselor to other service members, listening to their most personal concerns and providing careful, thoughtful advice. On late nights far away from home, living in a desolate and dangerous land, Clark listened as some men told him they were considering suicide. Others discussed troubling, but less important matters, such as how a spouse back home was spending their hard-earned pay.

Chaplains don't carry weapons, but because the military base was near the Iranian border, the Army considered this location risky and paid Major Clark accordingly. In addition to his basic pay, he qualified for hazardous duty and family separation pay, as well as housing allowances and other bonuses. As a result, he made good money: his pay and benefits totaled $98,000 annually, plus full medical and dental benefits, and 30 days paid vacation.

Eventually, Clark was transferred to the 188th Infantry Brigade at Fort Stewart, Georgia, as its mobilized brigade chaplain. But in June 2011, as the U.S. Army began to cut its forces, Clark lost his full-time position. Within a short period, his military income, including all of the bonuses and special pay, was gone. After moving back to his home in Tennessee, he was unable to find full-time work—even though he held two master's degrees.

Since his return home, Clark has worked nonstop, but makes far less than he did when he was stationed in Iraq. "I literally work every day of the week," he says. During 2012, he worked as a part-time music minister and also held part-time jobs as a painter, landscaper, and pressure washer that earned him approximately $27,000 a year. In 2013, he found a part-time job at Lowe's, the home improvement chain, which bumped his total annual income to approximately $38,000 a year.

To pay his bills, Clark needs to withdraw $500 each month from his savings. He lives a lean lifestyle, spending little on clothing and entertainment, but the drain on savings will continue until he begins to draw his military retirement pay in December 2014.

Clark's personal story illustrates the difficult financial issues service members face when they make the transition from the military to the civilian world. Service members who leave military service soon realize they are entering a new phase of their lives where jobs and pay are no longer guaranteed. The regular paycheck, the bonuses for combat pay, and the allowances for housing, all go away, as well as many of the medical benefits and other forms of insurance.

Fortunately, Clark managed his money well during his time overseas and while stationed at Fort Stewart, saving $4,000 a month and paying off his house and car. "Perhaps the most important financial lesson I've learned in my life is to pay-as-you-go," he says. "With the exception of my house and a couple of my past cars, I have saved for what I needed or wanted and then laid out the cash before taking possession. This way, I rarely find myself a 'slave to the lender.' Too many of my soldiers saw, desired, and acquired stuff. They repeated this cycle over and over and ended up living a fake lifestyle they couldn't afford."

Making the Transition

A service member needs to make several important decisions once he or she leaves military life. You likely will need to learn some new skills to start and grow in a new career; readjust to family and friends, and learn how to manage money and build wealth.

The skills needed to accomplish these goals will likely be different than the ones you learned in the military, especially when it comes to money. Many service members never had to manage their money and building wealth never crossed their minds. But outside of establishing your career and re-establishing ties to family and friends, it is one of the most important skills you will need.

It's not uncommon for veterans to face uncertainty when they return to civilian life. A survey released in August 2012 by Prudential Financial and the Iraq and Afghanistan Veterans of America (IAVA) found that 64 percent of service members say they experienced a difficult transition to civilian life. The survey also found that close to half of the veterans did not feel ready to make the transition largely due to employment and health challenges, but also the need to take time to decompress after service and "figure out what's next."

That's the $64,000 question—what is next? Of course, that's up to you. But when it comes to your financial life, I can get you started.

New veterans, particularly those post-9/11 vets, will need a financial plan in place to pay for living expenses and finance any major purchases once discharged. Think for a moment about this scenario and if it reflects your situation as you get set to re-enter civilian life:

★ Do you know where you will live?

★ Do you know where you will find work?

★ Do you know your monthly living costs, including all utilities and the costs of owning and operating a car or other transportation?

★ Do you have any outstanding debts?

★ Do you have any money saved from your time in the service? And, like the major from Iraq, do you know if you would need to dip into your savings for any short- or long-term needs?

If you know the answers to the first three questions, have no debt, and plenty of savings, I want to congratulate you; you are in very good shape. However, if this doesn't reflect your situation and if you are uncertain that your transition will be a smooth one, you are not alone.

Knowing the Pitfalls Ahead

I realize that you've given considerable thought to where you will live, whether you plan to go back to school, and what kind of money you will have available to make a major purchase—possibly a new car or even a new home. But I want to prepare you for a few possible pitfalls that may turn out to be obstacles to even the best-laid plans.

A lot of changes have occurred in the U.S. economy in recent years, and if you entered military service before 2007, most of the changes haven't been good. The unemployment rate is high, with several million people unable to find full-time work. More than four million individuals and families have lost their homes to foreclosure; more than five million have needed to work with their banks to modify their mortgage loans just to stay in their homes. Millions of others have seen their houses depreciate in value.

Veterans planning to save money by living at home with parents, relatives, or friends, may find that these loved ones have lost good jobs, experienced a reduction in income, or have lost their homes. If this is the case, it could significantly sidetrack your transition.

Bronze Star Winner Struggles With Finances

Nick Colgin is one of America's heroes. As I mentioned earlier, he served for 15 months as a combat medic for Bravo Company in the 82nd Airborne in Afghanistan. In one of his most memorable missions, after a French soldier was shot in the head, Colgin jumped out of a helicopter and ran to his side under heavy fire to save him. He and the Frenchman were pinned down for three hours, forcing Colgin to pick up a weapon and return fire until help came. Eventually they were rescued and, as a result of his efforts, Colgin received the Bronze Star for meritorious service.

Colgin joined the U.S. Army as soon as he finished high school and was discharged in August 2008. But this hero readily admits that, at least for a period, he was better suited for military life than many of the everyday financial challenges he faces as a civilian.

"I went into the military right out of high school. I'm not paying rent, I have insurance and any time I need to go to the doctor, I go," he says. "When I got out, I had never experienced buying groceries, paying rent or utilities." After four years of service where he regularly dodged gunfire, and during a period when his best friend from high school died in combat, he admits that many financial issues seem relatively trivial.

"You have a different value system," Colgin says. "I was in Afghanistan saving lives. In that world, as a medic, if I packed too many items and it weighed me down, I couldn't do my job and people would die. Now, it's still hard to realize that paying rent on time may have some long-term impact on my life. I'm wired to make decisions a little differently."

Colgin says he received no financial education during his military service, but wishes he had: "Out of everything, financial education and a resume would have been the top two things that would have made my transition easier." Even at age 28, Nick has only been paying rent for four years. "It's still kind of weird to get in the habit of doing that," he says.

Planning for New Expenses

Colgin did his best to plan for his transition with the information he had, but it wasn't enough. So one of the first pieces of information I want to provide you with is a list of expenses formerly covered by the Armed Forces that will become your responsibility. Knowing about these expenses will help you put together an initial spending and financial plan. These expenses include:

- ★ Transportation. If you lived on a military post, the places you visited most frequently were likely within walking distance. Upon separation from the service, you'll quickly discover that grocery and convenience stores, restaurants, and baseball stadiums are miles, not blocks, away.

- ★ Home Security. Large fences, military police, and other security measures protected the base where you lived during your days in the service. Although the enemy wasn't far away, you were safe inside the post. Now, at home, there is always the danger of a break-in and you may need

to pay for the installation of security devices and
a monthly fee to maintain security.

★   Clothing, utilities, meals, and recreation. In the
military, clothing, utilities, and meals are all provided by Uncle Sam. For exercise, you work out
regularly with other service men and women, so
there isn't a need for a gym membership or a personal trainer. But these personal expenses aren't
covered upon separation.

★   Television and more. If you were stationed overseas, you never paid for cable television and most
long-distance communication. If you want those
items now, you'll need to pay for them.

Begin at the Beginning:
Decide on Your New Personal Goals

Any overall financial plan begins by developing a monthly budget, and you'll need to include all of the items I just
listed. But before we do that, I want you to write down your
personal and financial goals. This is an important exercise
because it will help us build a personal financial action plan
to meet those goals.

Write down your goals in a document that you can look
at from time to time, either on a computer, mobile phone, or
notebook. At the end of this chapter, I've developed a worksheet where you can list your short- and long-term goals and
begin to develop your budget. Most veterans have their own
ideas about starting a new life, but few actually write them

down and have a game plan to achieve them. That's where my plan can help you.

Let's start by looking at your goals. It's likely that your goals fall into one of these categories:

★ Going to school (or back to college) to get a degree to help start a new career.

★ Buying a home.

★ Teaming up with one of your military buddies to start a business.

★ Returning home to a spouse and stable job, starting a family, and saving for the future.

★ Investing for a long-term goal, such as retirement.

We all know of military buddies who came back to the States and fulfilled a goal—as well as those who didn't. After returning from Iraq in 2008, my colleague Daniel Buffington eventually decided to use his savings from his military service to complete his college degree.

Back in 2007, as a member of the U.S. Army Reserves, Daniel was one of 30,000 troops called to serve in Iraq to rid the country of Al Qaeda and other insurgents. He and his wife only had 30 days to get their affairs in order before he was deployed. They spent several nights going over their bills and each due date. All of this happened just two months after the birth of their son, Andrew. But Daniel says that his financial planning has paid off.

"During my eight months of service in Iraq, I saved nearly $10,000," Daniel says. "When I returned home, I had some student loan and credit card debt, but I decided to use my savings to pay for my final two semesters of college and complete my degree in international business. The degree helped me get a new job in management. The job has worked out well; I was promoted within my first three years in the organization."

Although Daniel was surprised to get his orders to deploy overseas, he decided during his time in Iraq that he would spend his earnings wisely once he left the service. After having some difficulty finding a good job when he returned, he developed a specific goal—completing his college degree. It was also a goal that was realistic and had a specific time frame.

Setting SMART Goals

For the past several years, I've used a five-step method of goal-setting that has helped me accomplish many things. First used by George Doran, it's called the SMART process, with each letter representing one part of the process. As you begin to map out how you will achieve your personal goals, and pay for them, I would like you to use this process. Here are the five steps that you need to take:

S = Be Specific. Make sure that your goals are specific and not too broad in their scope. For example, if you want to become a teacher within your community, you need to set deadlines and complete some research. Here are some actions you need to take:

★ Find out exactly how long it will take to complete your degree and set a deadline to graduate.

★ Decide if you want to teach elementary school, or if you want to specialize in a particular subject, such as art or math.

★ Know what certificates are required.

★ Find out if there are jobs available where you want to teach. Talk to other teachers and school administrators now; don't wait until you graduate, only to find out that there are no jobs available and that there likely won't be any in the near future.

M = Measureable. You must have a way to measure progress and success toward each of your goals. It's easy to measure progress toward achieving a college degree. However, if you want to measure progress toward saving to buy a home or starting a business, you must put specific steps in place. And if you want to advance to the next level in your career in two years, you need to determine specific steps to help you achieve that goal.

A = Attainable. The goal you set must be one that you can reach by taking certain actions. For example, if you want to start a business, but you have no funds available, it will be difficult.

R = Realistic. Winning the lottery is not a realistic goal, but saving $5,000 over 12 or 24 months to buy a home is a realistic goal.

T = Timely. It is reasonable to have short- and long-term goals. The short-term goals should have a time frame of less than one year.

Once you have written down your goals, along with a timetable to implement them, you can develop a financial plan. Let me give you an example from my life.

Shortly after leaving military service, I decided on two short-term goals: to get out of debt and to buy my first home. Getting out of debt was my immediate, short-term goal, and I was very aggressive about meeting it.

I saved money by reducing my expenses and by using those savings to pay down my debt. For example, I moved to a residence closer to my job to save on gas, and lived with a roommate to save on housing costs.

Every extra penny went to pay off my credit cards, including my federal and state tax refunds. I worked overtime whenever possible and also worked the second shift, which increased my salary by 15 percent. By the end of the first year, I was debt free and had money for a down payment on my first home.

Assessing Your Current and Future Financial Situation

Now that you've written down your goals, you need to figure out a way to pay for them. And doing so will be the first part of the personal action plan that I will help you create. Let's start by assessing your current financial situation. Any assessment begins with basic needs, so you need to be able to answer the following questions:

★ Determine your housing costs, including utilities. If you can live with parents or a relative, you will significantly cut your overall living expenses.

If not, you and a friend may be able to split the cost of an apartment.

★ Determine your military benefits and incorporate any future benefits into your financial planning and monthly budget. As you know, veterans qualify for reduced interest rates on home loans; education, housing, and training benefits under the GI Bill; disability and medical benefits and pension benefits.

A quick note here: if you have decided to return to college as a full-time student, the new GI Bill will provide a living allowance that should cover much of your housing costs. Tuition is covered for any public university and $1,000 is allocated for books, giving veterans real financial incentives to attend college as a full-time student.

★ Combine your military benefits with your civilian income to develop a monthly budget. Make certain to account for medical expenses that may be covered for a period by Tricare.

★ Determine if your monthly income will cover your monthly expenses. If you find that there is a shortfall of income, you'll need to quickly find employment or look at other options to reduce your expenses.

Creating a Priority Spending Plan

Your priority spending plan will enable you to cover your expenses and allow you to save to pay for short- and long-term goals. Expenses will consist of two categories: items that you "need," such as housing and food, and those that you "want," which usually include entertainment, eating at restaurants, and weekends with friends at the ball game.

I'm going to help you set up the same kind of spending plan that credit counselors employ every day. Of course, every person will have a different budget and spending plan. A 22-year-old returning from active duty to live at home with his parents, will have a different income and set of expenses than a 32-year-old who serves in the reserves and is returning to a job and family. But my balanced spending plan can be adopted by anyone and be altered to fit your circumstances.

Here is a breakdown of your expenses, starting with the "big three" of housing, transportation, and food. The cost of housing includes utilities, such as water, heating, and air conditioning, as well as taxes and insurance. The costs for a car include maintenance, such as gasoline and oil changes:

Housing	38%
Automobile	15%
Food	12%
Total	65%

Because everyone needs a place to live, transportation, and food, these categories will always consume a large percentage of your income. For the remaining categories, I want you to allocate 5 percent to each one. These include clothing, insurance, medical, recreation, debt payments, and savings.

Finally, I've left 5 percent for a miscellaneous category. You will need money to pay for items that many people often forget to include in their budgets. These costs include everything from birthday and holiday gifts, furniture, haircuts, trips to the beauty salon, and anything else that doesn't fit into the other categories.

Now, let's put together a sample budget for a returning veteran. Let's assume that two young veterans have decided to get an apartment while they go back to school and work a part-time job. Each has an older model car to drive to work and school. Here's a monthly budget for each person:

Expense	Amount
Housing (rent, heating/air conditioning, water/sewer)	$600.00
Auto (monthly payment, gasoline, maintenance, repairs)	$300.00
Food	$400.00
Clothing	$100.00
Car insurance	$75.00
Health insurance	$50.00
Health club	$40.00
Monthly credit card payments	$50.00
Haircut/grooming products	$25.00
Savings	$0.00
Total Expenses	$1,800/month or $21,600/year

Therefore, each person must earn an annual minimum of $21,600, after taxes, to afford all of these expenses.

Here's another way to look at it: a person working 40 hours a week at $12 an hour would earn $480 a week. This would give them an annual salary of just more than $24,960. Assuming that she had to pay federal and state income taxes, she would have about the right amount of money to meet the expenses we've outlined previously.

As I mentioned earlier, the GI Bill provides post-9/11 veterans with full tuition at a public university, $1,000 for books and a living allowance, which will help cover housing costs. Because housing accounts for the single largest category in your budget, this makes it easier to attend college full-time, especially for someone who is single.

The living allowance differs based on where you live, with higher allowances for students attending college in large cities with high costs for houses and apartments. But if you can split the costs of rent and utilities with a roommate, the allowance may cover most, if not all, of your housing costs. It may not be easy to live this lifestyle for three or four years, but it is affordable. Still, you'll need to develop a budget and determine if you need a part-time job to cover your additional expenses.

For veterans opting not to enroll in college, this scenario shows how difficult it is to pay for even basic living costs, especially if you don't have a full-time job. It makes sense to find ways to cut expenses, including ideas that may seem drastic. For example, if owning a car appears too expensive, you may need to consider sharing a car or riding public transportation for a period.

The budget I've outlined is just one example, but it shows how easily expenses can exceed income and savings if you don't have a plan. If you are ever going to achieve the goals you've written down, you need to live according to your means. If you run the numbers and can't make it work, you may not be able to afford to rent an apartment with a friend. So you'll need to adjust your spending or make other living arrangements.

Finally, as part of this process, determine any issues that may stop you from paying your bills and living within your budget. Once you have found a job, the most likely costs you will face include transportation, housing, and child care.

Establish a Plan to Save Money

At this point, you have established your goals and developed a monthly budget to meet your daily living expenses. The next step is simple: you need to set up checking and savings accounts at a local bank, credit union, or other financial institution. These accounts will allow you to manage your expenses and begin to save toward the financial goals that you have set.

If money is tight, I know that you may wonder if this is the right move. But you need to save money to meet your goals, and a bank account is the best way to do that. Even if you start by saving 1 or 2 percent of your paycheck, it will add up. And as you get pay raises or come into additional money, you can increase the amount of money into your savings accounts.

Mechel's Tips to Build a Financial Action Plan

I want to conclude this chapter by summarizing all of the steps needed to begin building your financial plan. As I mentioned earlier, I've attached a worksheet at the end of this chapter that you can use to set up your plan. Here are the steps to take:

★ Write down your short- and long-term goals.

★ Write down your monthly income and expenses. Once you see your list of expenses, make sure to set up a priority spending plan based on "needs" vs. "wants."

★ If you don't have a bank account, open a checking and savings account and make regular contributions. Determine the amount you can contribute regularly that will help you reach your goals. For example, if you have decided that you want to buy a car and you need $1,000 for a down payment, you will need to save $83 a month for the next 12 months.

★ Put a plan in place to address any challenge that is preventing you from reaching your goals. For example, if your housing costs are too high, get an additional roommate or consider renting a room. Many homeowners want additional income and are willing to open their homes to returning veterans. If you need a car to get to work and school, see if your parents will help pay for a late model car.

Reconnecting Financially: Civilian Action Plan

Record your short- and long-term goals that you want to achieve upon separating from military service. Then, list your current income and expenses; then list your adjusted expenses in the "adjusted" column. Subtract your total adjusted expenses from your total income to determine whether your budget is balanced.

Personal Goals		
Short-term Goals		
Long-term Goals		
Income		
Net Pay:	Child Support:	
Disability/Pension/Social Security:	Other:	
Total Income		$

Expenses		
Expense	**Current**	**Adjusted**
Housing		
Rent/Mortgage	$	$
Other (taxes, insurance, maintenance, etc.)	$	$
Transportation		
Vehicle Payment	$	$
Gas	$	$
Parking/Public Transportation	$	$
Other (taxes, insurance, maintenance, etc.)	$	$
Utilities		
Electric	$	$
Gas	$	$
Water	$	$
Telephone	$	$
Other (sanitation, alarm, cell phone, cable, etc.)	$	$

Other Expenses		
Savings	$	$
Groceries	$	$
Medical	$	$
Personal Items	$	$
Credit Cards/Loans	$	$
Entertainment	$	$
Miscellaneous	$	$
Total Expenses	$	$
Total Income—Total Adjusted Expenses	$	

2

While You Were Deployed, the World Changed

It's been more than 20 years since I came home from war, but it's still hard to talk about the psychological and behavioral problems I experienced returning to civilian life. If you're coming home from Iraq or Afghanistan, or leaving the service for other reasons, know that hundreds of thousands of service members are going through similar adjustments.

When I came home from the Persian Gulf in 1992, my loving parents welcomed me with open arms. I was a heroine from a war where our Armed Forces pushed Saddam Hussein's Republican Guard out of Kuwait and back into Iraq. My parents beamed with pride as they talked about my service and accomplishments to all of our friends and relatives.

I was glad to be home, but shortly after I returned, I knew things were different. Like many of you, I enlisted in the U.S. Army right after high school, leaving the only town I had ever known. But my military service had molded me into a completely different person than the one who left home four years earlier.

I learned new skills and used them to help our troops on the battlefield. I had the opportunity to see and experience a new culture. During the times I left the military post, I made friends with some of the people in Sinop, Turkey, and became good acquaintances with several shopkeepers. I loved the culture and I will never forget the thrill of traveling to Istanbul, Ankara, and other parts of the country.

Maybe that's why coming home was such a shock. I had served my country honorably, lived in a foreign land, acquired new skills, and was filled with self-confidence. My hometown—a place where I had known everyone and every place—now seemed small and insignificant. All of the people I knew—neighbors and relatives, high school friends and teachers—had little knowledge about the war, military service, Turkey, or any of my other experiences.

The toughest part was that I was unable to connect with my parents. When I entered the service, I was a young girl with little to show besides a high school diploma. When I returned home, I was a 22-year-old woman, among the first women to serve during wartime in our nation's history. But as we tried to get reacquainted, it was difficult for them to understand, and for me to communicate, all of the personal growth that occurred during my time in the service.

As I settled in at home, my frustration grew over our inability to bridge our differences. Day after day, I became passive and withdrew into my old bedroom. With no job, no money, and no purpose, our conversations were short and tense. The joy of my homecoming quickly faded and, after six weeks, my mother was equally frustrated. In her calm, quiet manner, she told me that our living arrangement was not working out and she asked me to leave. I had to move out.

Not Ready for Transition

As the years have gone by, I've learned that my experience wasn't unique. Upon returning home, Nick Colgin was diagnosed with a traumatic brain injury. He spent a lot of time going to medical appointments and was forced to go on unemployment when he couldn't get a job. Eventually, he began to reach out to others for assistance. "Service members are trained to be tough and not ask for help," he says. "Many service members wait until it's too late. Don't be afraid to ask for help."

In this chapter, I'll talk about various kinds of changes that veterans may encounter during their return to civilian life. Once you recognize these unexpected changes, we'll look at how you can make some adjustments to your financial action plan.

Adapting to the Unexpected

Just as you would prepare for the unexpected on the battlefield, I want you to prepare for some potential changes upon your return home and the impact these changes can have on your financial life. In Chapter 1, we touched on some of these changes and how they could alter your goals and add to your living costs. Here are the most common scenarios:

★ Job Skills. As you try to transfer your military job experience to civilian life, the transition is often not smooth. Even though you may have experience in one field or acquired a new skill during military service, you may not meet an employer's qualifications. Most jobs require a degree, certification by an industry organization, or a state license.

★ Living Arrangements. As we've discussed, you may think that this is an easy decision to make, especially if you plan to move back home with your parents. But, as my story shows, your relationship with friends and family may be difficult to rekindle and lead to unforeseen problems.

★ Financial Shortfalls. It is common for veterans with medical disabilities to be forced to wait several months before receiving a decision from the Veterans Administration on their payments. It's also possible that these payments will fall short of your income needs.

★ Money Management. Many married veterans left the management of the family finances to their spouses while they were deployed. But some spouses had difficulty handling financial affairs, failing to pay credit card bills or spending a service member's bonus pay on unnecessary items. They may even have experienced their own money problems, either losing a job or seeing a cut in their hours and their pay.

Adapting to Obstacles Upon Your Return

In Chapter 1, I told the story of how Daniel Buffington saved money from his stint in Iraq and used it to finish his college education. But before making his choice to return to college, he faced key obstacles after returning home from military service and had to adjust his career goals and financial plans. He grappled with some of the same problems you may be facing.

Daniel left the military in 2008 and thought he would have no problems getting a job back in the United States. He had a strong resume, or so he thought: he had seven years of job experience, including a management role before leaving for his tour of duty. In the army, he was trained to manage the logistics of supply trucks moving between Kuwait and Baghdad during combat—a trip he made many times.

When he returned home, he applied for positions in logistics management and trucking at UPS and Federal Express, but didn't receive any job offers. He explains the problem: "Even though the country was in a financial crisis when I returned, the problem was not the lack of jobs, but translating what I did in the military to civilian life. You have to sum up a complex set of skills in a few lines and it's a struggle to explain it quickly and succinctly in a job interview."

There were also costs involved in training to get a commercial trucker's license, and he had just returned home to a wife and small child. So Daniel opted to return to college and finish his bachelor's degree—a decision he doesn't regret. But his case demonstrates the need for flexibility in your job and career choices.

Assistance for Veterans with Injuries

A large number of veterans returning home have suffered serious injuries or have been diagnosed with Post Traumatic Stress Disorder (PTSD). Of course, these veterans face much more serious obstacles and their transition back into civilian life is more difficult.

These veterans begin their financial journey back home by filing disability claims with the Veterans Administration (VA) and working closely with the VA to address their long-term health and medical issues. But many returning veterans also have additional financial needs.

There are several nonprofit organizations that try to help veterans in this situation. One of those organizations is my employer, ClearPoint, which is a nonprofit financial counseling organization. For veterans facing any financial hardship, speaking with a counselor at a nonprofit credit counseling agency will give you a foundation for your next financial move. Nonprofit credit counseling agencies don't provide financial aid, but they can speak with you about how to budget your money and guide you to other reputable organizations that can help provide financial assistance.

Since establishing a special counseling team made up of military veterans in 2011, ClearPoint has provided financial counseling to thousands of veterans and their families. One of the people on the ClearPoint military counseling team is Randy Satterfield. Randy served in the Air Force in the early 1970s and estimates that half of the veterans he has counseled have PTSD. He says that war time stress has an impact on their financial acuity.

"PTSD can be a primary cause of any financial hardship for 9/11 veterans of Iraq and Afghanistan. They simply can't process a lot of complex financial transactions," Satterfield says. Because of PTSD, he finds that married veterans are often better off financially because their spouses can handle all of the finances and usually have power of attorney.

How to Handle Financial, Emotional, and Behavioral Problems

Nick Colgin advises veterans experiencing any number of problems—physical, emotional, psychological, or behavioral—to seek help. Veterans with families also need to realize that these changes can affect children as well as adults. If you are experiencing problems, here are some strategies to consider.

Make requests for financial assistance through the Yellow Ribbon Registry Network and USA Cares. The Yellow Ribbon Registry Network provides veterans with a starting place to seek assistance. Individuals help veterans in need by donating cash, vehicles, and selling items on eBay. USA Cares provides financial assistance to help restore financial stability to a veteran's life. Financial assistance is not made directly to the veteran, but payments are made to mortgage lenders, utility companies, and other vendors. USA Cares attempts to help people at the earliest stage of financial problems to prevent future distress.

Here is the contact information for these two organizations:

Yellow Ribbon Registry Network: *www.registrynetwork.org.*

USA Cares: 1-800-773-0387 or *info@usacares.org.*

If you or a loved one has psychological or behavioral needs, here are some places for help and tips to consider:

★ Contact the local Veterans Administration hospital. The local VA hospital is the first place to reach out for help. They have specialists who are familiar with a variety of behavioral conditions.

★ Alert your child's school. Let them know that a family member has returned from the service and there may be changes in your child's behavior as the family makes adjustments.

★ Consider family therapy. If you can't handle the changes that are occurring, consider talking with a family therapist or counselor. Allow your child to see the school counselor, if necessary.

★ Meet with your Employee Assistance Provider. Many civilian employers offer Employee Assistance Programs, also known as EAP programs, as a benefit of employment. These programs may provide you and your family with the opportunity to speak confidentially with a counselor, free of charge.

Good News for College-Bound Veterans

Though adapting to civilian life may be challenging, some important institutions are investing heavily in helping veterans make the adjustment. Research shows that most colleges and universities are working more closely with veterans to help them thrive on campus, and these changes are having a major psychological impact on veterans returning to pursue their degrees.

A survey released in 2012 shows that 62 percent of 690 U.S. colleges offer programs and services specifically designed for military service members and veterans. The survey, "From Solider to Student II: Assessing Campus Programs for Veterans and Service Members," found that a majority of U.S. colleges and universities have a dedicated office to serve students who are veterans, provide counseling to assist those with PTSD, and have staff trained to assist with physical disabilities.

Rutgers University is one university that has invested in programs to help veterans succeed. After two students made a proposal to the University Senate in 2008, the university created an Office of Veterans Services. Two years later, it hired a former Army officer, retired Col. Stephen G. Abel, to run the office. At the time, there were 446 military veterans enrolled as Rutgers students.

Abel has a deep background in military service and administration, serving 27 years in the U.S. Army and as the New Jersey Deputy Commissioner for Veterans Affairs before coming to Rutgers. After arriving at the university, he developed a comprehensive plan to help veterans achieve their academic goals, while at the same time providing them with professional services to meet other needs.

He understands that the Post-9/11 GI Bill covers veterans' tuition and other costs for 36 months, giving them three years to complete a degree, or four years if they take summers off. "I recognized quickly that veterans don't have the luxury of taking a semester or two to figure out if they don't like their major," says Abel. "After 36 months, their GI benefits stop. It's critical to get them good advice in their first term."

To accomplish this goal, Abel asked Mike Beals, the vice dean of the College of Arts and Sciences, to have one of his academic advisers work at the Veterans Center one day a week. Beals saw the need and decided to make a counter proposal; he would personally serve as the academic adviser for all military veterans that attend Rutgers.

"His offer was much more than I asked for," says Abel. "About 50 percent of our veterans are enrolled in arts and sciences, so we have the second highest ranking person in the college giving us his support. Now, if a veteran is near the end of his 36 months and needs a course to graduate, Mike can help the veteran get access to the course."

Tutoring for veterans is also critical, particularly in languages where the veteran may not have taken a class for several years. And not just any tutor. In 2011, Abel developed a tutoring program matching a veteran with a tutor for one semester or even longer, depending on the veteran's needs. This long-term working relationship has made a big difference, Abel says: "Not long ago, a Navy veteran who took French in high school went to his first class at Rutgers, and everybody in the class was speaking French. He came back to Veterans

House and told us that he wouldn't make it and needed to get out of the class."

Rather than take this route, Abel connected with a student group called "Are You For Troops?" that helps veterans with academic issues. The group sent Abel to the French department for help. During Abel's visit to the department, a new exchange student from Paris overheard the conversation and volunteered to tutor the Navy veteran. He proved to be an excellent tutor, helping the veteran earn an "A" in both semesters.

Because many veterans need access to a variety of professional services, Abel has decided to bring those professionals to the veterans on campus. A variety of specialists, ranging from psychologists to mental health counselors, keep part-time offices in the Office of Veterans Services building. In addition, a full-time employee from the Veterans Administration has an office there. As a result, the office serves as a one-stop shop for a veteran's needs.

These kinds of programs demonstrate that many colleges and universities understand the psychological needs of veterans returning to campus life. I will address other aspects of returning to college in Chapter 5 as part of understanding how all of your military benefits fit into a financial plan.

Impact on Your Personal Financial Action Plan

If you incur an unexpected problem during transition, it may have an impact on your financial life and the personal financial action plan I want to help you build. If you are going through a personal crisis, an injury is preventing you from working, or a government agency is causing a cash flow problem, it is important to act rationally and not panic. Making a bad decision could take you months, or even years, to recover financially.

If you have a financial emergency, here are some immediate "do's" and "don'ts":

★ Do not get a payday loan, a title loan, or other short-term, high-interest loans. These loans are incredibly expensive and can be difficult to repay.

★ Instead, as painful as it seems, start your search for funds by asking family and friends for short-term help. It is much easier to work with people you know and trust than an online payday loan company.

★ Consider selling major assets that aren't critical. This includes your car, particularly if you can get to work with an older model car or with public transportation.

★ Carefully consider taking out a personal loan, using a credit card or borrowing from a 401(k) or other retirement savings plan. The latter option is a last resort.

Setting Up an Emergency Fund

For the rest of your life, there will always be a need for funds to pay for an unplanned expense. Your car may break down; your child may have an accident and need to go to the hospital; you or your spouse may suddenly lose a job, causing a significant reduction in your household income.

To pay for these unplanned expenses, everybody needs to start and build an emergency fund. Once you have your priority spending plan set, it's time to start contributing to an emergency fund. Here are some steps that you can take:

★ Set up a checking or savings account where you can access the money quickly and easily in an emergency. If you want to shop around, several accounts offer no fees, and little or no minimum balance requirements. Visit *www.bankrate.com* to compare rates and information from various financial institutions.

★ Set a goal. I recommend having enough money to cover at least three to six months of living expenses, which will allow you to pay the mortgage or rent, utilities, food, gasoline, and other essential expenses. If that's too aggressive, start slow; consider setting an initial goal of $1,000. But if you lose your job, you'll need to have money available to cover your expenses until you can find a new one.

★ Make steady contributions. Re-evaluate and adjust your spending plan to allow for regular contributions to your emergency fund, even if it's $10 per pay period.

Mechel's Personal Tips: How to Build an Emergency Fund

Saving money is not easy and millions of Americans are living proof because they live paycheck to paycheck. Many people need to look for opportunities to find a few dollars here and there to squirrel away. Here's how I contribute to my emergency fund:

★ I build the contribution to my emergency fund into my monthly budget; that is, I treat it as one more expense, which allows me to budget for it each month. Start with $10, $20, or $50, but make a regular contribution.

★ Take advantage of different savings programs offered by various banks. For example, Bank of America will transfer small amounts of money from a checking to a savings account when you make a purchase. In effect, they "round up" your purchase to the nearest dollar. If an item costs $1.29, the remaining 71 cents may go into your savings account. Over a year, this can amount to several hundred dollars.

★ I help my daughter build her savings by matching the amount I add to my own savings. When she receives money for her birthday or another holiday and deposits it into her savings account, I do the same and add a zero. If she saves $5, I save $50.

★ If you receive a bonus or a tax refund, use all or part of this windfall to begin your emergency fund, or add to it.

★ I also make it difficult to take money out of my account. When I began saving, I opened an on-line savings account and automatically sent $200 into the account each pay period. If I wanted to make a purchase, I had to walk into a bank branch and cash a check because I didn't accept a debit or ATM card with this account. This makes it nearly impossible for me to take money out of the savings account.

Now it's your turn; list some ways you can start building an emergency fund today. Write down at least three things you will do immediately to either begin or increase your emergency fund.

1.

2.

3.

3

Dealing With Debt

On the day the World Trade Center was attacked in 2001, Matt Colvin joined the U.S. Air Force. He trained hard to serve his country, learning to translate information about enemy communications and jam those communications while he was aboard a special cargo plane. He was deployed to Afghanistan twice, supervising a crew of linguists who could understand Arabic. In 2005 and 2006, he flew on nearly 100 missions as part of Operation Enduring Freedom.

Colvin rose to the rank of staff sergeant during his six years of military service. As a sergeant, Colvin was able to take classes and receive presentations about finance, and there was also an office on the base that offered financial advice. But Colvin never felt that the information he received was adequate. "The members of my squadron were given recommendations about how to handle our money, but it was never a focus of our education," he says.

Colvin left military service in 2007 with $10,000 in savings. But after arriving home, he took a three-month vacation and promptly blew it all. Colvin explains how it happened:

I spent my money on anything and everything; bar tabs, barbeques, traveling, and whatever else I liked at the time. I spent money on friends and family. I loaned money that I never got back, and I just generally did what I wanted, when I wanted. I blew the money because I was reckless; I was living in the "now" versus thinking of the future. I had just spent six years in one of the most rigid systems in the world, and I was ready to let loose, which I did at the expense of all the savings I had accrued. I always believed there was time to save money tomorrow, and I wanted to enjoy the good times and the people now.

After his three-month vacation, Colvin moved to New Jersey to join a new skateboard company started by one of his childhood friends. He and the other new owners lived and worked in a warehouse to build their dream company. As Colvin says:

We lived and worked out of the nearly 5,000 square foot space, which was fully equipped with an indoor basketball hoop, a full bar, our production facility, and living quarters. It was like living in *Big*, the movie starring Tom Hanks, all while building a company. For the first couple of months I slept on the shop floor, constructing my "bedroom" each night after work then tearing it down again to work the day.

Thank God, I had a comfortable air mattress and a wood stove that kept the brick cold warehouse tolerable. It was definitely roughing it, but I loved every minute of helping to build something lasting. We ate a lot of pasta in those days, but did what was necessary to keep things in the company moving.

But with the startup in need of cash, Colvin didn't receive a paycheck for six months. So he needed to borrow money just to buy necessities. Says Colvin:

I applied for a $10,000 line of credit, but I only qualified for $5,000. I lived a meager lifestyle in the first year of joining the company, and I only took money out when truly necessary. The card definitely saved my life during that time and allowed me to focus on how I could help the company. Even without splurging, I racked up debt pretty quickly to pay small bills, to purchase items for the company, and just to live. I applied for a second card without a good interest rate and maxed that one out over the course of 12 months. It was how I had to live to maintain the dream of being a part of building something lasting. I would do it all over again, but I would have asked more questions and planned better.

Colvin eventually left the startup in 2009 to enroll in college and finish his bachelor's degree, which he completed in 2012. Unfortunately, the credit card debt stayed with Matt for many years. "I can't recall how long I paid minimums, but it was for years," he says. "It's taken me six years to really knock down the amount of debt I had accrued. I still have some of that credit debt looming over me, but it's not nearly a burden as it had been in the past."

Colvin's story shows how even a responsible veteran working to build his dream can fall into debt, which can take years to pay off.

The $250,000 Car

Many service members return home with debt, whereas others never even have to leave the country before they take out a big loan and take on payments that they can't afford. One of my favorite stories about how service members rack up debt comes from a car dealer just outside of Fort Hood, Texas, one of the U.S. Army's largest military posts.

The car dealer sells sports cars and young military men with money in their pockets make up his client base. To demonstrate his selling skills, he likes to talk about one of his favorite sports cars that has earned him a lot of money through the years. "How much do you think this car is worth?" he'll ask somebody. A person looks up and down at the car, which doesn't look any different than any other used sports car. Most people would guess the cost at between $15,000 and $25,000.

A good guess, the dealer says. But no, this is a special car; it's worth $250,000.

You know that amount can't be right, so you ask him to explain. The car is worth $250,000 because he has sold the car to new service members over, and over, and over again. Young men, who are 18 or 19 years old, with money to spend, see the car and make the purchase. Sooner or later, the car needs repairs, or they tire of making the payments, or they can't make the payments because they've spent their money on other things. When that happens, he repossesses the car, sticks it back on his lot, and sells it again.

Daniel Buffington says he witnessed similar scenes when he was stationed in Iraq. At Camp Victory, just outside of Baghdad, automobile and motorcycle dealers sold vehicles to service members right on the base. If I'm a car dealer, I can't think of a better opportunity to earn money; access to tens of thousands of young men and women shuttling back and forth between the United States and Iraq, money burning a hole in their pockets, and new, shiny vehicles sitting right outside their barracks.

Service members accumulate debt for a variety of reasons. And a debilitating amount of debt can make you worry and take your mind off your mission. That's why high levels of debt are among the leading causes of service members losing their security clearance—the Armed Forces can't take a chance on someone in debt making a decision that could hurt our country and our security.

High levels of debt can stop you from accomplishing all of those goals we set down in Chapter 1. If you don't have enough money to pay your debts, it can stop you from accomplishing other goals, too, such as getting a job and purchasing a home.

Now it's time to tackle your debt. In this chapter, I'll lay out debt reduction strategies for both one- and two-income households. We don't want your debt to stop you from accomplishing your goals, so we'll also fit our strategy to pay down debt into your new personal action plan.

Don't Get Bamboozled:
How to Pay Off Your Debt

Because millions of people owe more money than they can repay, a new industry has sprung up: one that says it can help people pay back their debt. If you're heavily in debt for the first time and looking for help, you will soon notice a nearly non-stop barrage of online, television, and radio advertising.

The people in these ads will claim that they can pay off your debt fast. Others will say that they can help you pay off less than the full amount that you owe. Of course, that's how they get your attention; if you believe they can help get you out of debt quickly, you'll probably give them a call.

These ads can be effective because they help fill a void of information. Despite the fact that millions of people in the United States need help in reducing their debt, there are few places to turn and get objective, solid advice.

Advertisers also know that most people don't want others to know about their financial problems. We will seek advice from friends and family about love, where to go to church, and where to get a job. But no one wants their friends or family to know that they are in debt. As a result, many people end up turning to a person or company they've never met to rid them of tens of thousands of dollars in debt. Does that really make any sense?

If you are in debt and need help, you have three choices: I call them the good, the bad, and the ugly.

The Good

There are three good ways to work off your credit card debt:

★ Develop a plan to gradually pay it off yourself. In a moment, I will show you how that works.

★ Contact your creditors and attempt to secure a new, lower interest rate.

★ Work with a nonprofit credit counseling agency to develop a debt repayment plan that will lower the interest rates on all of your credit cards and eliminate late fees and other penalties. These organizations have worked closely with credit card companies for decades and have helped hundreds of thousands of people reduce their payments and pay down their debt.

The Bad

There are several options that are risky and don't get you any closer to paying down your debt. These choices include online payday lenders, title companies, and debt settlement companies. My advice is to stay away from all three. Let's examine the debt settlement industry.

The Federal Trade Commission (FTC) did an extensive investigation of debt settlement firms and issued a report in February 2011. The agency concluded that debt settlement can be very risky, have a long-term negative impact on your credit report and, in turn, hurt your ability to obtain credit.

It concluded that debt settlement firms may claim they will negotiate with your creditors to reduce the amount you owe, and that they can arrange for your debt to be paid off for a much lower amount—anywhere from 30 to 70 percent of the amount you owe. For example, if you owe $10,000 on a credit card, a debt settlement company may claim it can arrange for you to pay off the debt for less, say $4,000. Some debt settlement firms may also claim to be nonprofit.

However, according to the FTC, there is no guarantee that the services debt settlement companies offer are legitimate. There is also no guarantee that a creditor will accept partial payment of a legitimate debt. In fact, if you stop making payments on a credit card, late fees and interest are usually added to the debt each month. If you exceed your credit limit, additional fees and charges can also be added. This can cause your original debt to double or triple. All of these fees will put you further in the hole.

Creditors are not obligated to negotiate the amount a consumer owes. However, they have a legal obligation to provide accurate information to the credit reporting agencies, including your failure to make monthly payments. That can result in a negative entry on your credit report. And in certain situations, creditors may have the right to sue you to recover the money you owe. In some instances, when creditors win a lawsuit, they have the right to garnish your wages or put a lien on your home.

Finally, the Internal Revenue Service considers any amount of forgiven debt to be taxable income. For example, if you owe $10,000 and a debt settlement firm is able to cut the amount to $5,000, you will still owe taxes on the other $5,000. This amount must be declared as income when you file your taxes. So, by the time you pay off the firm and pay your taxes, how much have you really gained?

For all of these reasons, my advice is to stay away from debt settlement firms.

The Ugly

If you have a large amount of debt and very little income, you may need to file for bankruptcy. It is the last option to consider because of its long-lasting impact, but it is an option.

There are two primary types of personal bankruptcy: Chapter 13 and Chapter 7. You will need to speak with an attorney to determine your best option. Whereas fees vary depending on the complexity of each case, the costs to hire a bankruptcy attorney can run as high as $2,500. Here are some basic facts about each type of bankruptcy.

Chapter 13 allows someone with a steady income to keep their property, including a house with a mortgage or a car where payments are still owed. In a Chapter 13 bankruptcy, the court approves a repayment plan that allows you to use your future income to pay off your debts during a three-to-five-year period and keep your property. After you have made all the payments under the plan, you receive a discharge of your other debts, such as your credit card debt.

In a Chapter 7 bankruptcy, all assets that are not exempt from the bankruptcy may be sold or turned over to your creditors. Exempt property may include automobiles, work-related tools, and basic household furnishings. You must wait eight years after receiving a discharge in Chapter 7 before you can file again under that chapter. Before you file a Chapter 7 bankruptcy case, you must satisfy a "means test." This test requires you to confirm that your income does not exceed a certain amount. The amount varies by state and is published by the U.S. Trustee Program at *www.usdoj.gov/ust*.

Both types of bankruptcy have some benefits: you may get rid of unsecured debts and stop foreclosures, repossessions, garnishments, and utility shut-offs, as well as debt collection activities. Both also provide exemptions that allow you to keep certain assets, although exemption amounts vary by state. And, unlike debt settlement, any debt forgiven in bankruptcy is not taxable.

However, personal bankruptcy usually does not erase child support, alimony, fines, taxes, and some student loan obligations. And, unless you have an acceptable plan to catch up on your debt under Chapter 13, bankruptcy usually does not allow you to keep property when your creditor has an unpaid mortgage or security lien on it.

If you file for bankruptcy and follow all of the rules, your debt will be discharged. This is a court order that says you don't have to repay certain debts. However, bankruptcy information (both the date of your filing and the later date of discharge) can stay on your credit reports for 10 years. It can make it difficult to obtain credit, buy a home, get life insurance, or sometimes get a job. Still, bankruptcy offers a person a fresh start.

Good Option No. 1: Paying Off the Debt Yourself

If you have a steady income and earn enough money to make more than the minimum monthly payments, it isn't difficult to begin paying down your credit card debt on your own. But you will need a plan and you must have the discipline to stick with the plan for at least several months, and possibly more than a year.

Most people suffering from heavy credit card debt have an average of five credit cards. They feel trapped because they don't believe they have the ability to pay off their credit debt within a reasonable period of time. People in this situation not only fail to reduce their credit card debt; they actually see the amount they owe increase because of high interest rates.

There is one simple strategy for digging yourself out of this credit mess. Choose one credit card—probably the one with the lowest amount owed—and begin making payments that are larger than the minimum amount. The goal is to quickly reduce the amount owed until the card is paid off while continuing to make the minimum monthly payments on the other credit cards. Here is an example:

	Amount Owed	Minimum Payment	Pay This Amount
Credit card No. 1	$500	$15	$75
Credit card No. 2	$1,250	$40	$40
Credit card No. 3	$3,000	$70	$70
Credit card No. 4	$4,000	$90	$90
Credit card No. 5	$5,000	$110	$110

By paying $75 monthly on the first credit card, you will be able to pay it off within just a few months. Once you have four credit cards left, take the $75 you were paying on the initial credit card and add it to the amount you've been paying on one of the remaining four cards. Of course, you want to continue to repeat this process until your credit card debt is substantially reduced or eliminated.

Good Option No. 2:
Ask Your Creditors for Help

Despite what you may think about credit card companies, there is one important truth to always remember: they want to be paid. The recession and tepid U.S. economy of the past few years has meant unemployment and reduced income for millions people, which forced credit card companies to eat hundreds of millions of dollars in loans. They would rather get some money than no money.

You have nothing to lose by asking your credit card company for a lower rate, especially if you have suffered a recent hardship. But you will have to be persistent.

Start with the telephone number on the back of your card or your statement. Keep good records of your debts, so when you reach someone at the credit card company, you can explain your situation. Your goal is to work out a modified payment plan that reduces your payments to a level you can manage.

Good Option No. 3: Work With a Nonprofit Credit Counseling Organization

If you are unable to pay down your debt or negotiate a lower payment, I recommend speaking with a nonprofit credit counseling organization. Reputable nonprofit credit counseling agencies have been around for more than 50 years and one of their primary services is to help people pay down their credit card debt. There are nearly 100 organizations around the country with the Consumer Credit Counseling Service (CCCS) brand and each will help you review your finances at no charge.

A counselor will review your monthly income and expenses, make recommendations to reduce your spending and possibly free up enough cash to make your credit card payments. There is no charge to speak with a counselor and you can find the nearest CCCS organization by calling the National Foundation for Credit Counseling or visiting their Website, *www.nfcc.org*.

If a budget review doesn't free up enough cash, the counselor may be able to work out a long-term repayment plan with all of your credit card companies. Referred to as a Debt

Management Plan, the nonprofit will work with all of your creditors to arrange new, lower interest rates.

The plan provides several benefits, but the two major ones are a substantial savings in the amount of money you will owe and a plan to pay off your debt. If you are paying an interest rate of 18 percent or more, the nonprofit can often lower your interest rates on each credit card. This change will eliminate your debt much quicker.

However, you need to understand that not everyone will qualify for a repayment plan. If possible, credit card companies want to receive a full payment, so you will need to show that a hardship situation exists and that your current income isn't enough to make the regular, scheduled payments.

If you do qualify, you will make a single, monthly payment to the nonprofit organization, which will distribute the funds to all of your creditors. The nonprofit will charge a monthly fee that usually does not exceed $50 each month.

For the veteran seeking to reduce credit card debt, a Debt Management Plan will help you get your finances back on track. It will also stop creditors and collection agencies from calling and help you begin to rebuild your credit score.

Mechel's Tips

If you have credit card debt, I've provided you with three sound options to begin repaying your credit cards. Examine all of your options and choose the best one for you. And remember, there is no charge to call and speak with a nonprofit credit counseling organization.

The achievement of your goals hinges on your financial health, so it's imperative that you get your debt under control. You must implement a plan to pay down your debt.

If your current budget does not enable you to do this, you must make some significant changes. Very simply, you must earn more money and drastically reduce your expenses. Do not hesitate to speak with a financial counselor to get more detailed advice.

Use this credit card debt reduction worksheet to prioritize your credit card debt. List the name, interest rate, balance, and minimum payment for each of your credit cards. Determine how much money you can allocate to pay down your debt each month and begin to pay down the credit card with the least amount owed.

Credit Card Name	Interest	Balance	Minimum Payment	Additional Amount

4

What If I Can't Pay My Mortgage?

Falling behind on your mortgage payments and facing the possibility of losing your home to foreclosure is one of the most difficult financial situations for any family. But solutions are available.

Ronald W., who served as a First Sergeant in the U.S. Army, and his wife, Vicki, were facing foreclosure among a long list of financial issues shortly after he left the military in June 2012. The couple was three months behind on their mortgage payments and four months behind on one of their car payments. Vicki had cancer and was unable to work, and the couple had been turned down for financial assistance from various relief organizations.

On top of all of these problems, Ronald, who suffers from PTSD following his service in Iraq, was unemployed for approximately one year. So the couple turned to their mortgage company for a loan modification.

In recent years, mortgage companies have been working with many homeowners to reduce their monthly payments—in effect, modifying their mortgage loan—to help them stay in their homes and avoid foreclosure.

The couple's initial application was rejected by their lender, so they turned to ClearPoint for help. After collecting a variety of documents, including bank statements and W2 forms, a team of specialists at the nonprofit worked with the couple and their mortgage company to resubmit their application. Six months later in November 2012, Wells Fargo modified Ronald and Vicki's mortgage loan, reducing their monthly payment by approximately $500 each month and saving their home from foreclosure.

Research Shows Many Vets Face Housing Issues

Although there are several established ways to attack credit card debt, mortgage loans are more complex, making it tougher and more time consuming to get help. Let's examine this problem and the possible solutions.

Data show that the vast majority of homeowners who fall behind on their mortgage payments have either lost a job or experienced a significant reduction in household income. And though many of these people have found new jobs, a good number are earning less money than they did at previous positions.

Research about people who come to ClearPoint for help tell the story well. More than 80 percent of veterans and active duty service members who received credit and housing counseling from ClearPoint in 2012 were homeowners.

Approximately 54 percent of veterans between ages 30 and 39 cited unemployment or reduced income as the primary reason for needing counseling; for those between ages 40 and 59, it was more than 60 percent.

Unfortunately, most of these veterans also had a significant amount of credit card debt. The average veteran owning a home owed between $13,000 and $15,000 in credit card debt. When you add in a car payment and other basic living expenses, most homeowners have trouble meeting their regular expenses pretty quickly.

Most people with a solid emergency fund can withstand a major financial hit for a few months. But many people haven't set aside enough money and even those who have can be squeezed within a short period.

Potential Solutions for Homeowners

Here is my first piece of advice: if you lose your job or another significant income source, don't resort to borrowing money to fill the void in income. Instead of addressing their overall financial health, many people panic and turn to credit cards, while others begin to pilfer their 401(k) and other retirement accounts. I strongly advise you to consider solutions that attack the root of the financial problem.

There are reasonable solutions for people who want to continue living in their homes. And, despite what you may have heard, many banks and mortgage companies are willing to work with homeowners to restructure your mortgage loan. Here are a few of the common solutions for people concerned about losing their homes.

Hardest Hit Funds

Homeowners who lost jobs in 18 states and the District of Columbia may qualify for funds that help them make their mortgage payments and avoid foreclosure through the federal government's Hardest Hit Funds program. State housing finance agencies are working with unemployed homeowners in these states to help people as they search for new jobs. States have until 2017 to utilize more than $7 billion in funds.

Loan Modifications

In recent years, banks have been willing to modify, or rework a mortgage loan to lower interest rates, and potentially lower your payments. This means that they will revise the old agreement you signed when you first purchased your home and give you a new agreement. Although not everyone will qualify for a loan modification, this solution has helped millions of homeowners keep their home.

However, getting approval for a loan modification is often not easy and it can take several months. The bank or mortgage company will examine your hardship and current financial status to determine if you qualify—in effect, they want to know if you can still make your monthly mortgage payments, even if they lower the monthly payment by hundreds of dollars.

The bank will review your new monthly income and expenses to determine if your hardship is legitimate and whether to offer you a loan modification. If they agree, you will be required to make payments for a few months on a trial basis to see if you can make your full payment on time before they offer you a permanent loan.

Plain and simple, if you want to keep your home, a loan modification enables you to do that. But make certain that you understand the details of any new loan agreement. A loan modification changes the terms of the loan. This means that not only does the amount you pay change, but the period of time to repay the loan may start over.

For example, if your original loan was for 30 years and the monthly payment was $1,000 at a 6 percent interest rate, the new, modified loan may change these terms. The advantage is that you will now pay a lower interest rate, even as low as 2 percent, which could lower the monthly payment from $1,000 to $600. And this is one of the primary reasons to consider a loan modification.

However, for some loan modifications, the lower interest is only temporary, and will usually last no more than five years. Within a couple of years, the interest rate will begin to rise. In our example, a rise in the interest rate from 2 to 3 percent will likely mean a $50–$100 increase in the monthly payment. The interest rate may increase one or two more times before it levels off.

One disadvantage of a loan modification is that the clock may start over on the length of the loan. This means that your new loan is for 30 years. So if you want to stay in your home and own it, you must make regular payments for the next 30 years.

Of course, many people don't plan to stay in their current home forever. A loan modification allows you to keep your home and make lower payments and, as the economy recovers and housing prices rise, the value of your house may also increase. If this happens, many people may still be able to sell their home and possibly make a profit.

Short Sale

If you lose your home to foreclosure, your credit score will be severely damaged, limiting your ability to get credit for major purchases in the future. Even if you and your family get new, good-paying jobs and recover financially, banks and other creditors may decide not to loan you money or may charge extremely high interest rates.

A short sale allows a homeowner to sell their home for less than the amount owed. Here's how a short sale may work: you may have bought a house for $175,000 by making a down payment of $25,000 and taking out a loan for the remaining $150,000.

But when the economy worsened, home prices fell. Consequently, the house may no longer be worth $175,000. Instead, it is now valued at only $135,000. Even if you made regular monthly payments for several years, you still owe more money than the home is now worth.

If you have lost a job or another source of income, a short sale is one way to sell your house and avoid foreclosure. A short sale will still damage your credit, but the impact is less severe compared to a foreclosure. When you recover financially, your ability to purchase a car or home at reasonable interest rates are better than if you experience a foreclosure.

But completing a short sale can be a long process and you will need help from your bank. You will need to list your house and attempt to sell it at a fair market price for 90 days. You will also need to hire a real estate agent who will have the house appraised, and the home will be listed to sell at a price similar to homes of the same size and quality in your neighborhood and surrounding area. If you cannot sell the home at this price, you will need to get the bank's approval to sell the home for less money than the appraised value.

Even after all this, it will be up to the bank or mortgage company to decide if they are willing to go along with this strategy. If you find a buyer willing to pay less money than the appraised price, the bank will receive less money than the amount of the loan. And if you have not been making mortgage payments during this whole period, they will need to decide what works best for them: selling a home for less money than the loan or foreclosing on the property.

Here are some additional tips when considering a short sale:

★ When you list your home for sale with a real estate agent, make certain that the real estate agent is experienced in dealing with short sales. They will help you work through the process with your lender.

★ Short sales do not happen quickly with most lenders. After your home has been up for sale and there have been no prospective buyers, you should plan on the short sale process to take several weeks and possibly months.

★ Even if your Realtor is helping you through the short sale process, stay in contact with your lender. It's recommended that you check with your lender at least every 10 days to see if they need any further documentation from you.

★ Once your lender approves you for a short sale, you need to get a Release of Lien. This document releases you from any obligation to pay the difference in the amount from the sale price of the home and the balance you owe. You do not want the lender to come back to you for the difference.

★ Know the tax consequences of any short sale. Ask your lender if they will report the short sale to the Internal Revenue Service because any amount of debt that is forgiven could be subject to taxes. The difference between the actual loan amount and the home's sale price could be reported on a 1099 form as income, which would require the homeowner to pay taxes. The Mortgage Forgiveness Debt Relief Act of 2007 ensures that homeowners who complete a short sale will not be responsible for the amount forgiven by the lender, but this law was only in effect until December 31, 2012. You may want to discuss this with your accountant, tax professional, or certified public accountant.

Strategic Default

In recent years, many people with a home worth less than the amount they owed decided to simply leave or "walk away" from the home rather than continue to make the monthly mortgage payments.

Even if they could afford the monthly payments, these homeowners believed that their home had turned into a bad investment. They decided that it would be years, if ever, before they would be able to recoup the value in the home. This action is known as a "strategic default." It means that the homeowner decided to intentionally default on their mortgage loan payments.

For many homeowners, this may have turned out to be a good decision. For example, there are homeowners in California who believed they would have suffered financially for the remainder of their lives if they held on to a home they bought before the housing crisis.

And there are other homeowners who used the threat of "walking away" to negotiate a new mortgage agreement with their lender that allowed them to stay in the home at a lower price. If you own a home that is still "under water," or you already have "walked away" from a home, you need to know the following information:

★ Your mortgage company may try to file a lawsuit to recover the amount owed on the home.

★ Homeowners with unpaid home equity loans or second mortgages may also face legal action if they "walk away" from an unpaid mortgage or conclude a short sale.

Be Wary of Scammers

Some businesses and law firms offer to help homeowners renegotiate their mortgage loan and reduce their payments. It doesn't make sense to use any of these companies because the same services are available at no cost from a nonprofit housing counseling agency approved by the U.S. Department of Housing and Urban Development (HUD). I want you to be aware of several "red flags" that should warn you that a business is likely a scam:

★ **Guarantees.** Be wary of any company that offers a guarantee of stopping foreclosure regardless of your circumstances. Keep in mind that verbal promises and agreements relating to your home are not usually binding, so a guarantee in an ad or from their representative may be meaningless.

★ **Up-front fees.** Some companies charge a fee before reviewing your situation or making a single call on your behalf. Beware of any attempt to collect payment from you before providing a service.

★ **Redirected payments.** Do not agree to make payments to a third party. Some scams involve having the homeowner pay a company with the promise that they will make your mortgage payments. If they fail to do so, you have lost your money and may still wind up in foreclosure. Always make payments directly to your mortgage company.

Consumers need to be especially cautious of any attempts by a company to stop them from communicating directly with their lender, with an attorney, or with a housing counselor. They need to carefully read every document and fully understand what they are signing. Never allow the company to complete the paperwork for you or pressure you into signing a document you have not thoroughly reviewed.

Mechel's Tips

If you have fallen behind on your mortgage payments, or you are afraid that you will, there are several places where you can get help. Here are some places to start:

★ **The Homeownership Preservation Foundation.** I highly recommend starting with The Homeowner's HOPE Hotline, which is available 24/7. You can call 1-888-995-HOPE (4673). This toll-free telephone number is operated by The Homeownership Preservation Foundation (HPF), an independent national nonprofit dedicated to helping distressed homeowners navigate financial challenges and avoid mortgage foreclosure.

Homeowners in distress will be routed to one of several nonprofit housing counseling organizations certified by HUD. A counselor will speak to you about your situation and help you understand all of your options. You may also start an online counseling session at *www.995hope.org*.

★ **Hardest Hit Funds.** In 18 states and the District of Columbia, there is help available for people who have lost their jobs or are severely underemployed.

Thousands of people have already received funds to help them make their mortgage payments as they looked for new jobs. This program will be available through 2017. Go to the U.S. Treasury Department's Website to find out more detailed information.

★ **Home Affordable Modification Program (HAMP).** This is the federal government's loan modification program that may lower your monthly mortgage payments in order to make them more affordable and sustainable for the long term. If you occupy your home as your primary residence, contact your mortgage servicer as soon as possible to begin the HAMP evaluation process.

★ **Home Affordable Refinance Program (HARP).** Homeowners who are making all of their payments on time, but have experienced a decrease in their home's value, may have the opportunity to refinance. Through a refinance under HARP, Fannie Mae and Freddie Mac will allow the refinancing of mortgage loans that they own or that they guaranteed in mortgage backed securities. To see if your mortgage is eligible for a refinance, visit *www.makinghomeaffordable.gov/get-assistance/loan-look-up/Pages/default.aspx.*

5

How Veteran's Benefits Fit Into Your Financial Plan

When I bought my first home in 1996, I didn't know that veterans qualified for a VA (Veterans Affairs) Home Loan. After I had already selected a house and got approved for a loan, my real estate agent just happened to ask me if I was an Army veteran. If he hadn't, I never would have known that I qualified for special financing.

With a VA Home Loan, the interest rate on my mortgage loan was almost two points lower compared to the market rates at the time. The lower interest payments were quite helpful; they've saved me tens of thousands of dollars over the life of the loan. And the money I saved every month in lower payments went into my savings or was available for other essential expenses.

Today, these benefits for veterans are still extremely good. A VA Home Loan allows qualified buyers the opportunity to purchase a home with no down payment. There are also no monthly mortgage insurance premiums to pay, limitations on buyer's closing costs, and an appraisal that informs the buyer of the property value.

When I left the military in 1992, I didn't know that I could receive any benefits other than paid college tuition from the GI Bill. There were many Persian Gulf War veterans who didn't receive financial counseling and most of us didn't understand all of the benefits we were entitled to receive. Fortunately, over time, I've found out about my benefits, and I've been able to build them into my overall financial plan.

Of course, I utilized the GI Bill to help pay for my college tuition. I went to work for IBM, which had a tuition assistance program that also helped pay for my degree. I was lucky that IBM had this type of program because, at that time, the GI bill did not cover all of my tuition. I went to school full time during the day and worked the second shift at IBM to avoid getting swamped by student loan debt.

With careful planning, veterans can afford major purchases and sock away money by taking advantage of key benefits. Even today, when I tell people I'm a veteran, I receive discounts on a variety of goods and services. I recently bought a new pair of running shoes and qualified for a 10 percent discount. If you are a veteran but do not have a veteran ID card, just show your DD-214 and you will qualify for military discounts. Even better, you can obtain a form called a Certificate of Eligibility for Veterans Driver's License/ Identification Card from the VA. Turn in this authorization form at your local Department of Driver Services to obtain a free driver's license and identification card. Your license will show your veteran status and can be utilized for discounts at local retailers.

In this chapter, I will provide you with a summary of all of your benefits, plus a number of trusted nonprofit organizations that can provide financial counseling and assistance.

What Are My Benefits?

The first order of business is finding out which benefits you are qualified to receive. Any person affiliated with military service is listed in the Defense Enrollment Eligibility Reporting System, better known as DEERS. On the Internet, visit *www.military.com/benefits*, and the DEERS link should appear. Once on the Website, go to the eBenefits section and create a login to gain access to the site.

The process to create an eBenefits account will take a few minutes to complete. Once you enter all the required information, the Website will need to verify it before you receive access. The eBenefits Website will link to a database tied to the credit reporting agencies about your credit history. Once you answer questions correctly that are tied to this information, an account will be created.

The eBenefits Website will enable you to check on a variety of military benefits. You'll be able to access information on medical and disability claims in the Veteran's Administration database, apply for additional benefits, add dependents or a spouse, and update bank information.

If you are not in DEERS or if the information there is inaccurate, contact a DEERS Support Office (DSO) representative to make the needed changes. You can speak with a DSO representative at 800-538-9552.

As you begin to research other benefit programs, there are specific departments and agencies that can help you. Here is a list of the most important ones:

★ As we've mentioned, the Department of Veterans Affairs is probably the single most important government agency for a variety of needs. You can reach the Veterans Affairs office at 800-827-1000 or at *www.va.gov*. I would suggest setting aside a day to go to the local VA office and speak with a representative about getting registered. Once registered, you can find out about various benefits you are qualified to receive. Always take your DD-214 and two forms of picture identification, keep all records and information you are given, and stay organized.

★ The U.S. Department of Labor has career centers to help military personnel make the transition to civilian employment. Specialists in this department can help you translate your military service jobs and achievements into civilian terminology.

★ Transition Assistance Program (TAP). This program is designed to help veterans with all aspects of returning to civilian life. It provides guidance about employment opportunities, local resources, and help with legal and financial questions.

★ Disabled Transition Assistance Program (DTAP). If you were released from service because of a disability or you believe you have a disability that will qualify you for the Vocational Rehabilitation and Employment program, you should visit the Website *www.vet-trans.com/TapOffice* for more information.

The most common benefits for most veterans fall into two categories: disability and medical benefits, and the GI Bill. Each veteran will have different situations, so here is some general information to get you started regarding these benefits.

Disability and Medical

You can receive monthly compensation for injuries incurred during military service. You may also qualify for continued health coverage upon separation for you and your family.

Unfortunately, it has been well documented that many veterans are waiting several months for their disability claims to be processed. Veterans Administration Secretary Eric Shinseki has said that the VA would eliminate the backlog by 2015 and make sure that none of the claims takes longer than 125 days to process. During this waiting period, many veterans do not have the financial means to pay for many essential items, including food and shelter. Some of the nonprofit organizations listed later in this chapter may be able to assist you during this period.

The VA claims process can take a long time. But understanding the process will help you better manage your expectations and help expedite the process.

You can file any claim in eBenefits on the DEERS Website. Once you complete all of the documents needed for your claim, the VA begins its review. They will want evidence to support any claim, so submit any evidence at the time you file. Don't be surprised if the VA comes back with questions and requests for more documents during the application process.

If you are filing for disability for the first time you should speak with a veteran's field service officer who can guide you through the process. If you have filed for a claim and have not heard back or received any information as to the status of your claim, you may want to engage a Veteran Service Organization (VSO) to help work the claims process for you. The form you will need is called Appointment of Veterans Service Organization As Claimant's Representative. You will need to authorize the VA to disclose your medical records and any other treatments you received while in the Armed Forces. This person will be acting on your behalf so it is critical that you understand this process and what's involved.

Engage Your Representative

For other questions about health care benefits, contact your OEF/OIF/OND representative if you served in Operation Enduring Freedom, Operation Iraqi Freedom, and Operation New Dawn. If you do not have a representative, contact your local VA health center or go online and start an application there at *www.va.gov*. If you do not have access to a computer, you can call them directly at 1-877-222-VETS (8387).

No matter what your status is, you will need to fill out form 10-10EZR for health benefits. The government has also extended coverage for personnel who served during the three periods I referenced previously, providing them with five years of health care benefits after military service ends. Those who qualify for disability compensation may have up to 12 years after their service ends to apply for vocational rehabilitation. For more details, go online and read about the variety of programs in the *Federal Benefits for Veterans* guidebook which you can find online and on the eBenefits Website.

Planning to Attend College

Going to college to obtain a degree is a high priority for many veterans. A 2012 Prudential Financial study found that 44 percent of veterans are going to school full- or part-time, and two-thirds say they are using the Post-9/11 GI Bill. The student population rises among those who are unemployed (53 percent) and those not seeking work (70 percent). People in both of these categories are more likely to name "lacking education" as a barrier to employment. Veterans have high educational aspirations; among those who only have a high school degree, three-quarters hope to achieve a college degree or more (74 percent).

By now, if you have done your research, you know that the Post-9/11 GI Bill will pay for most, if not all, of your college education. In 2008, Congress expanded the benefits beyond the old GI Bill program for military veterans serving since September 11, 2001. Beginning in August 2009, recipients became eligible for the full cost of any public college in their state. The new bill also provides a housing allowance based on where you live and attend school, a $1,000 stipend for books, and many other benefits.

Two years later, Congress expanded the education benefits even further. Effective October 2011, a new housing stipend was provided for those attending college online, giving them $714.50 per month if they are enrolled as full-time students.

All of these benefits will help a veteran earn a college degree. But the reality remains that, even with tuition and housing paid for, it's still difficult financially to be a full-time student and pay for daily living expenses. And it's even more difficult if the veteran is married with a family. So let's start by making sure that you understand all of your possible benefits and how they fit into your financial plan.

To understand all of your benefits, take a look at Iraq and Afghanistan Veterans of America's (IAVA) GI Bill Checklist at *http://newgibill.org/getting_started*. Following those steps should help clarify the process and allow you to build some predictability into your GI Bill experience. If you are curious about the costs covered by the GI Bill, go to IAVA's New GI Bill Calculator or FAQ section at *http://newgibill.org/calculator/* and find out how the GI Bill can help you achieve your education goals.

As I mentioned earlier, the two largest categories of veteran's benefits are medical and disability, and the GI Bill. But there are plenty of other benefits for which you may qualify. Here's a brief description of each with information about how to find out more:

★ **Home Loans.** For veterans that want to buy a home, the Veterans Administration guarantee to lenders allows them to provide you with more favorable terms, including:

- No down payment, as long as the sales price doesn't exceed the appraised value of the home.

- No private mortgage insurance premium requirement.

- VA rules limiting the amount you can be charged for closing costs.

- You do not have to be a first-time homebuyer.

★ **Homelessness.** There are also programs for veterans who feel they may be headed toward homelessness due to their inability to keep their home. For those people in that situation you can go to *www.va.gov/homeless/index.asp* where assistance can be provided.

★ **Health Care and Life Insurance.** You may have access to your local Veterans Administration hospital for ongoing medical issues. And there are life insurance benefits that you may want to utilize upon separation from active duty service.

★ **Additional Benefits.** You may qualify for other benefits, such as accrued leave, burial benefits, PX or commissary access, transportation benefits of your household items to your new residence, and pension benefits. In addition, there are work related and career placement services, vocational rehabilitation programs, as well as pension and retirement services. To find out more, you can begin by contacting the Veterans Affairs Department at 800-827-1000 or at *www.va.gov*.

Nonprofit Organizations for Veterans

Whether you find help or not from a government agency, there are a number of nonprofit organizations that specialize in providing support for veterans and their family members. These organizations all serve a specific purpose, or target a specific group of veterans, family members, or survivors.

Here are some of the organizations that ClearPoint Credit Counseling Solutions works with which provide support, including financial assistance, to veterans:

★ **Iraq and Afghanistan Veterans of America (IAVA).** Help is provided in the areas of health, education, employment, and community building. Visit *www.iava.org* for more information.

★ **VeteransPlus Yellow Ribbon Registry Network (YRRN).** This is a one-stop resource for a variety of needs, including helping a veteran apply for a financial donation to pay for a specific need. VeteransPlus has worked with more than 185,000 active duty service members, veterans, and their families since it was founded in 2001. Visit *www. registrynetwork.org* to learn more about YRRN.

★ **Military OneSource.** For up to six months following the end of tour of service, retirement, or discharge, this organization is a free service provided by the Department of Defense with a broad range of services. Military OneSource addresses concerns such as money management, spouse employment and education, parenting, relocation, deployment, and the concerns of families with special needs.

★ **Military Spouse Corporate Career Network (MSCCN).** This organization offers no-cost employment readiness, vocational training and job placement services, and other services for spouses, homeless female veterans, and caregivers of those wounded in war. Visit *www.msccn.org* for more information.

★ **Veterans of Foreign Wars of the United States (VFW).** This organization has been instrumental in helping veterans with disability claims who have served during overseas conflicts as well as improving VA medical care for women veterans. They act as advocates to ensure that veterans and their families receive all the benefits they are entitled to. Visit *www.vfw.org* for additional information.

★ **Other Organizations.** Military veterans and their families have access to a variety of other resources through support groups associated with the VA. For more information, contact your local family service center or military chaplain, or visit *www.va.gov, www.oefoif.va.gov,* and *www.vfw.org.*

6

Spending and Savings Habits That Will Last a Lifetime

During military service, every aspect of our financial life is cared for by Uncle Sam. The U.S. Army pays for our food, clothes, and housing. Whenever we want anything, we walk a short distance from the barracks, so we don't need a car. The post is secure, so we don't need to worry about criminals breaking into our homes and stealing our property.

Veterans appreciate how our government and military leaders take care of service members. Our pay is stable and the benefits are unmatched.

Unfortunately, during my four years of service, I didn't learn how to manage the money I was earning. There were no classes or guidelines about how to spend wisely and save my paycheck. And, at such a young age, I simply didn't realize the importance of saving for emergencies or building wealth.

This lack of financial knowledge hurt me for some time after I was discharged. I made plenty of mistakes. Not only did I buy a car that I couldn't afford, but I didn't have a plan about how to find stable employment. When I realized my mistakes, it was time to leave my parents' home and find my own place to live. That's when I decided that I needed to start from scratch and develop a plan to take control of my financial life.

In Chapter 2, I described many of the emotional and psychological challenges that many of us encounter after returning home from war. But once we understand these issues and their impact on our finances, we need to take action. That's what I did, so let me help establish some spending and savings habits that will benefit you for the rest of your life.

Spend Wisely. Save. Repeat.

Let's examine your current financial situation. You've started to develop a financial action plan. You've established your short- and long-term goals; put together a budget that takes into account your income and expenses, and determined your strategy for paying down debt. For veterans facing more serious problems, such as foreclosure or bankruptcy, you now know some steps to avoid or soften the impact of these problems.

Now comes the tough part: you must execute your plan. It's one thing to make a list of your financial goals, whether it's earning a college degree, buying a house, or saving money for retirement. It's another thing to fulfill those goals and make them a reality.

No matter what goals you've established, there will always be a limited amount of income to fulfill your goals.

Everyone has limits, whether they make $40,000 or $200,000 a year. So, one of the best ways to make certain that you have enough money to fulfill your goals is to simplify your lifestyle. This will enable you to spend money wisely, save what is leftover, and put you on a path to reach your financial goals. Here's what I mean:

- ★ I want you to think differently and make new choices about the items you buy. You will also need to do a better job of evaluating when and how you purchase items.

- ★ Realize that more is not always better.

- ★ Slow down and take the time to care about things that are most important to you.

Really, That's How You Want Me to Live?

I know that this advice doesn't sound like a lot of fun. And you may think that simplifying your lifestyle means that you can't spend money and enjoy yourself. You can, but you will need to make some wise choices and some trade-offs. Otherwise, you won't reach your financial goals.

When I talk to my friends about simplifying their lives, this is what I hear: "Does this mean I can't go out to a restaurant or a night out with friends?" And I always hear this one: "Why do my old Army buddies always have money for cars, to go to clubs and bars, or travel on weekends, but I don't?"

Well, guess what? If you want to reach your goals, it may mean making some changes to your lifestyle and spending habits. When we dedicate ourselves to a goal, whether it's going to school to complete a degree, or working 10-hour days to get a bonus or promotion, we need to make some sacrifices.

Do Your Friends Really Have Money?

I know what you are thinking: "Am I the only one who doesn't have any money?"

It's easy to come to that conclusion. You see and hear about your friends having a good time. When you speak to them or view their activities on Facebook, isn't everyone always having fun? They post their photos from parties or trips; they are smiling, holding a beer or glass of wine in one hand, and hugging a boyfriend or girlfriend. They are showing all of their friends that they are having the best time wherever they are. If only you could be there!

But think about what you don't see. You don't see people posting comments about their crushing credit card debt. You don't get phone calls from friends telling you how they are concerned because they don't have enough money to make the next rent or house payment. If a collection agency is calling them every day, looking for a payment, you don't hear about it.

And does anyone ever post a comment on Facebook or Twitter about borrowing money from their family or friends to pay their bills? We know that they don't.

The numbers don't lie. You know your income, and if you've done a realistic budget, you know how much money is needed each month to cover expenses for essential items.

So you know how much is available for entertainment, travel, and even simple expenses such as eating out at a restaurant. Just because people are buying new cars or spending late nights at the club, it doesn't mean that they can afford it. Appearances can be deceiving.

How to Live Simpler: A True Story

Jason Spangler and his wife, who live in the Atlanta suburbs, asked for help from ClearPoint in 2009 to pay down their debt. They had eight credit cards with interest rates ranging from 8.99 percent to 29.99 percent. Jason tells how they got into financial trouble:

> Like many who have fallen into the plastic trap, it was a combination of things. For my wife and me, it was not earning enough money while we were trying to maintain a lifestyle beyond our means. This problem was exacerbated by medical expenses that pushed us into using our credit cards more and more.
>
> My wife has type 1 diabetes. She was diagnosed just months before our wedding. We really didn't have great health insurance when we first married, but what's worse is we were simply ignorant about how health insurance works, so we did not plan or budget for our out-of-pocket expenses. And we paid for some of the expenses for our honeymoon to Alaska on credit.

Working with ClearPoint, Jason and his wife developed a plan to pay down their credit card debt. Over the next three years, they paid more than $800 each month while also adopting a simpler lifestyle to fit their financial needs. Jason continues:

> We made our first payment on May 2009, and made our last payment July 2012, almost three years to the day. We learned how to manage our money finally by living on a budget, plus we were able to increase our income for a time.
>
> We are working on paying off our student loans now, and at the same time saving up an emergency fund of at least three months of living expenses. We also began giving money to support our local church. Giving money to charity further changes your perspective on finances. Our pastor says that giving money away changes you more than the one receiving it.

Jason and his wife have decided to start a family, and gave birth to their first child in the summer of 2013. They did some financial planning to reduce their medical expenses. Jason says: "One of our goals was to come out of the delivery room with no huge hospital bills. So we put money into our health savings account to cover our expenses. The old 'us' would have racked up untold amounts of credit card debt instead."

Taking Steps to Live a Simpler Life

Any change in lifestyle begins with a plan, as well as a commitment, to change your behavior. Making small changes in how you think about purchases, and in your actions, can go a long way in helping you live a simpler lifestyle. Here are some basic guidelines to follow.

Adopt a new way of thinking about the products and services you purchase. To stretch your limited income, you need to think about "wants" vs. "needs."

We know from setting a monthly budget that costs for food, housing, and transportation will account for the majority of our monthly expenses. We need food, clothing, and housing; we don't need the latest flat screen television, the most complete package of programs and movies available from our cable television provider, or the latest home stereo system. As you evaluate your short- and long-term goals, make sure that you spend your paycheck to cover items that help you achieve those goals.

Before you purchase an item, here are some simple questions to ask:

- ★ Do I really need this item? Is it important to my life or work?

- ★ How will this item make my life better? Will something of great importance or value be lost if this item is not purchased?

- ★ What other opportunities will I pass up if I spend my money on this item?

- ★ Have I done my research to get the best price and quality before making my purchase?

- ★ Finally, can this item be bought at a later date without having a detrimental impact on my life?

Spend Money on Needed Improvements

The next basic step is to upgrade only when necessary. For many people, upgrading to better quality has become a way of life when it comes to cars, furniture, electronics, and appliances. The problem is that these items cost hundreds, even thousands of dollars, every time you make a purchase.

Living simply doesn't mean that it's wrong to upgrade. But it does mean thinking about the financial impact of any major purchase. For example, everyone needs a reliable car to get to and from work. If you maintain a new car properly, it can easily last 10–12 years and saves you tens of thousands of dollars compared to buying a new car every five years.

Unlike my first car, my current car is six years old. When it was paid off, I celebrated by upgrading with a new navigation system. Even a small upgrade like this one makes it feel like a brand new car.

I have continued this same ritual with the past two cars that I've owned. I make sure to get new tires when needed and have regular maintenance performed according to the car's manufacturer. I could buy a luxury car, but I like having an extra $400 a month that I can use toward my long-term savings goals and entertainment.

Living a simpler life doesn't mean you'll be unhappy because you can't purchase new things. It will actually free up money to spend on the items most important to you instead of those that bring short-term value or happiness. Here's a good example.

Is Taking Tae Kwon Do Class "Living Simply"?

I recently bought a one-year membership to a Tae Kwon Do studio for me and my daughter, and it's the best money I've spent in a long time. I'm engaged in a fun activity with my child, getting regular exercise, losing weight, meeting new people, and learning Korean. My 9-year-old is learning a new skill and gaining confidence and self-esteem. What could be better?

This expense does not fit the strict definition of a "need." But parents with young children need to find activities where we can build lasting bonds with them. At the end of the day, that's one of the best investments any of us can make—and still have fun.

As I considered buying the two memberships, I did my homework, weighing the impact of this new expense on my monthly budget. I reviewed my expenses and determined that I could reduce costs in other categories while still contributing at the same rate to my retirement account, as well as my flexible spending accounts for health and day care. I review my regular expenses monthly to see if adjustments can be made to food, gasoline, utilities, and other costs, and I determined I could keep those in check.

Next, I negotiated the best membership price possible. The regular price for a one-year membership was $130 a month, but I took advantage of two weeks of free, private classes to check out the quality of the program. After that, I spoke with the owner about costs and negotiated a price of $108 a month. I did my research, understood the expense and the impact on my budget. Once I was satisfied that the benefits clearly outweighed the costs, I wrote the check.

Although the class is good for my mental, physical, and emotional health, there are also hidden financial benefits. If my daughter and I weren't taking this class, we'd likely be spending money shopping, dining out, or on another activity where there would be little financial return. Instead, we are spending quality time together doing something that we both enjoy.

Other Reasons to Live a Simpler Life

In addition to achieving your financial goals, living more simply can help alleviate stress in our personal and professional lives.

It's easy to feel overwhelmed by the demands of life. I know people who believe that they only have time to go to work, go home and take care of their children; handle all of the household chores and go to sleep. And they still have trouble making ends meet financially.

These people don't maintain a balance between work and other aspects of their lives. They work eight to 10 hours every day on the job, then logon to their computers or check e-mail from their mobile phones at home and work some more. There is little time left for relaxation, exercise, hobbies, or fun with family and friends.

Living simply also means there are smaller payments and less maintenance on the items you buy. Many people make choices based on ads that try to reduce the cost of a purchase, such as $55 a month for a new television, $60 a month for a cell phone, or $100 a month for new furniture. But when you add all these small payments together, the amount can become stressful. By reducing your dependence on these purchases, you will begin to reduce the stress that comes along with making numerous payments.

Utilize Items on Hand

The final step to living simply is to take an inventory of your existing possessions. This will help you determine if the items you already own will meet your needs before purchasing anything new. Make a realistic plan to get organized. Then, assess the items that already exist and how they can be fully utilized.

Have you ever gone to a friend's house and marveled at how beautiful everything looks? The new furniture is pretty, and the entertainment center and game room are eye-popping.

In contrast, your home may include a sofa you've had since college and other rooms need updated. These are the moments where you need to stop and think about the debt you could incur if you buy all new furniture, lamps, rugs, and other items.

Instead, look at your entire house and consider moving or mixing and matching existing items before buying anything new. Recently, I moved my sofa from the living room to the family room just to get a new feel in the house. I've also changed a spare bedroom into a home office, and then changed it back to give my daughter some additional space.

It would have been easy to buy new furniture for my living room. Instead, I switched paintings and moved furniture to give the house more space.

Here's another idea: my parents, brother, and sisters like to buy or give furniture to each other. I've given two sofas to a sister and she's sold one. It's one way we save money and change the "look and feel" of our homes without spending thousands of dollars on new furniture.

Mechel's Top Five Tips for Simple Living

To help you get started, I am going to provide you with five basic tips that I have used to simplify my lifestyle. Some of the tips go back to when I returned home from Turkey more than 20 years ago and others are those I started more recently.

If you can incorporate even a couple of these recommendations into your everyday spending and savings habits, you will reduce your spending by thousands of dollars a year. This money can be applied toward your goals—college, buying a house, or saving money to start a business.

1. Limit food purchases outside of the home. This includes everything from purchasing coffee at the fast-food restaurant in the morning to buying lunch and snacks in the afternoon at work. Buying food at the grocery store for all of your meals, as well as any snacks you want to take to work, will help save money. Savings for this tip: if you save more than $100 each month, that's more than $1,200 a year.

2. When shopping for food, buy store brands. Don't be fooled by the packaging; whether it's soup, frozen vegetables, orange juice, spaghetti, or cereal, the ingredients are often the same. Savings for this tip: if you can save $50 each month, that's $600 a year.

3. Shop or ask for lower rates on just about everything. You can reduce costs for auto insurance, heating bills, cell phone, and credit cards with a simple phone call. Do some comparison shopping on auto insurance rates and call your carrier to see how you might reduce premiums. Your cable company may be able to lower your monthly bill or offer you a special promotion for a period of time that can result in savings. Savings for this tip: if you can cut $120 each month, that's $1,440 a year.

4. The biggest savings may call for a big sacrifice. Getting rid of premium television channels on cable or satellite could save at least $10 a month. If you get rid of cable altogether, it would put more than $100 back in your pocket monthly. You can still enjoy your favorite shows by subscribing to Netflix and Google TV, and using Redbox to rent cheap movies. Savings for this tip: if you can cut $110 each month, that's $1,300 a year.

5. Save more money for your long-term goals by raising your 401(k) contributions by 1 percent each year. As the economy improves, investment

returns may improve. For a person earning $50,000 annually, 1 percent is $500—approximately $10 per week. Think about the amount of money you will earn over several years, as well as the tax benefits.

Track Your Emergency Savings

Use this worksheet to set and track your savings goals. Monitor your progress by using the savings tracker to record each deposit and transaction. Remember, if you need to access money in your emergency fund to handle an unforeseen event, adjust your spending and develop a plan to replenish it as soon as possible.

My Savings Goal

3 months living expenses $ _____

6 months living expenses $ _____

Other: _____ $ _____

My Savings Tracker

Date	Transaction		Balance	Notes
	Type	Amount		

7

Where Do You Want to Be in 5 Years?

How do you plan to get ahead financially? Have you decided on your goals and mapped out a plan to achieve them? If you want to achieve your goals and build long-term financial security, it's essential to take this next step. To get you started, let me tell you how I'm going about accomplishing my long-term goals.

I bought my ranch-style suburban home in 2008, and my top long-term financial goal is to pay off the mortgage loan as quickly as possible. For motivation, I think about the benefits of being debt free and having all of that extra money once I don't have a mortgage payment.

When I visualize how I can invest all of my new cash, and grow my wealth, it motivates me to reduce my spending on unnecessary everyday items and do whatever I can to reach this goal.

I also have a dream for all of that new capital, and that motives me, too. Once I pay off my mortgage, I want to purchase a second home. I often go on vacation to Hilton Head Island, South Carolina, and recently I spent time with my Realtor looking at homes for sale. There are some good deals available on foreclosed property that will make a good investment and provide my daughter and me a permanent vacation home.

The dream of purchasing this property has spurred me to put together a long-term plan to pay off my mortgage. As part of my plan, I am allocating $2,500 a year to extra mortgage payments. Coupled with my regular mortgage payment, I will have my house paid for by 2022.

To accomplish these goals, I've decided to scrutinize the amount I spend on routine, everyday expenses, eliminate or reduce the cost of those items, and apply any savings to my mortgage payment. Here are some examples of how I am watching or reducing my expenses:

★ I've eliminated long-distance telephone service from my home phone.

★ I keep a detailed file of all of my receipts for day care and medical expenses, which are eligible for reimbursement as part of my employer's flexible spending plan. I spend about $4,000 annually on these items. When I get reimbursed for these expenses, I take this money to make extra payments on my mortgage and other debt.

★ I organize all other expenses and deductions that may help me reduce my federal and state income taxes, ranging from mortgage interest to charitable contributions. Like many people, each year I usually receive a sizable refund and this money is also used to make additional payments on my mortgage.

Do you see what is happening? By implementing my strategy, I'm making progress toward my long-term goal. It's so much easier because each day I get up thinking about the benefits of paying off that mortgage, becoming debt free, and having the capital available to increase my wealth and improve my life.

It's Time to Set Your Long-Term Goals

By now, you've made some important decisions. You've established your short-term goals and you're on the way to fulfilling them. Younger veterans have found a place to live and may have decided to go back to school. Those who are 30 and older may want to buy a house and start a family. And veterans who own a house and have children are focused on saving for their child's college fund or for their own retirement.

I began working at IBM when I was 23 years old, two years after leaving military service. At first, my earnings helped pay for my college education so that I didn't have to borrow money. After I received my degree, I established my first set of long-term goals: to buy a house and begin saving for retirement. During this time, I was able to save money for my first home while also contributing 15 percent to my 401(k) retirement savings account.

To help decide your most important long-term goal, consider this question: if you had $10,000, what would you do with it? Here are your choices:

★ Pay off some or all of your debt.

★ Invest in your retirement account.

★ Start a college fund for your child.

★ Put aside money in your emergency fund to handle unexpected expenses.

These are all good options. But the question makes you focus on the goal that is most important to you. It also makes you realize that it will take much longer, often years, to achieve a long-term goal. To make certain that you don't lose patience or get sidetracked, you need to follow a process to establish the right goals and set a timetable to achieve each one.

The Process

The process for setting long-term goals has one major difference compared to the short-term. It involves a commitment to save, invest, and manage your money.

The first objective is to identify and commit to goals that inspire you—much like my dream of buying a vacation home. Whether it's getting your child into college, starting a business, or moving overseas to live near a European or Asian city where you were based, this goal should be something that you are passionate about. Of course, it will help if your goals also build long-term wealth.

When setting your long-term goals, use these three steps:

1. Start with the end result in mind.
2. Put your goals in writing.
3. When obstacles appear, adjust your plan.

The End Result

Achieving a long-term goal requires commitment. You need to visualize the end result to stay inspired to save money and make choices to support your goal. For me, the goal of owning a vacation home is appealing for several reasons. It's in a small resort town near the ocean that isn't crowded (at least not during the summer). I can enjoy the beach and all of the amenities of the town. It's a get-away from a large city, a good investment, and a place to share with my daughter.

All of these things make me feel good and inspire me to save money to achieve my goal. So find that goal that motivates you to take control of your money and turn your goal into reality.

Write It Down!

If you haven't already done so, write down at least one long-term financial goal and envision how your life will be different if you can achieve it. Let's go back to my goal of paying off the mortgage on my primary home and buying a vacation home.

Here's how my life will be different. My house will be paid off and I will own an asset worth at least six figures. I will then buy a second home where I can live near the ocean.

Lastly, I will be able to enjoy my vacations and have a home where I can retire.

Goals are best achieved when they are specific and can be measured. After you write down your goals, you need to put a plan into place that includes a timetable. For example, if you want to buy a new home or save for your child's college education, you will need to set aside hundreds of dollars each month.

Next, pursue this savings goal with a laser focus. Find ways to reduce your spending so that you can hit your savings target every month. Most importantly, determine if there are any other actions you can take that will motivate you to achieve your goals.

A Success Story: How One Veteran Achieved His 5-Year Plan

One of my favorite success stories is how Daniel Buffington developed a long-term career and financial plan after serving in the U.S. Army. Within five years of receiving his honorable discharge in 2008, he completed his college degree and is now a mid-level manager at a national nonprofit organization. He has also developed and put into place a personal financial action plan that is allowing him to achieve his financial goals.

Let's take a look at how Daniel did it.

Daniel's Career and Financial Plan: Part 1 (April–December 2008)

★ Complete bachelor's degree, giving him more future job opportunities.

★ Use part of $10,000 in savings earned during Iraq service to complete college degree.

★ Pay off $2,500 in credit card debt.

Daniel received his orders in July 2007 and spent nine months in Iraq, leaving in April 2008. Before serving overseas, he was working as a manager for a debt collection company. After leaving the military, instead of returning to that position, Daniel decided to complete his bachelor's degree. He went to school full-time for two semesters and used part of the $10,000 he and his wife had saved from his military pay. In addition, the couple decided to pay off the $2,500 they owed in credit card debt.

Daniel's Career and Financial Plan: Part 2 (January–July 2009)

★ Saved $15,000 and started a new investment account.

★ Started college savings fund for new son—contributes $500/month.

★ Paid $5,000 in debt on two cars.

★ Continued to make regular mortgage payments.

Even before Daniel received his college degree in late 2008, he began interviewing for management jobs. But with the U.S. economy at the start of a protracted recession, he had difficulty even getting interviews. Then, he learned that a company with a contract for the U.S. Army in Iraq needed a manager to coordinate truck routes and other logistics—a job that was similar to the one he held just months before with the Army.

He didn't want to leave his wife and young son for a second overseas stint, but it was the only job he could find and the money was good—about $7,500 per month after taxes. Daniel took the job for six months, returning home when it became too dangerous to stay. Although he had not advanced his career at this point, the pay allowed him to reduce the debt on his house and car. It also enabled him to fulfill two key financial goals: start a college savings account for his son and a new individual investment account.

Daniel's Career and Financial Plan: Part 3 (August 2009–July 2010)

★ New job gets career on track, but staring salary is low.

★ Child support and new car force Daniel to dip into savings to pay monthly bills.

★ Employer offers 401(k) and matching contribution, allowing him to invest money tax-free.

Returning home for the second time in mid-2009, Daniel entered another period of rapid change. His career received a boost after he found a new job at Bank of America. Unfortunately, the strain of military deployment and lack of stability took a toll on his family life, and Daniel and his wife decided to divorce.

Despite the new job, Daniel's financial plan took a hit during this period. He didn't have a high salary and the divorce meant that he needed to pay child support. In addition, his car was breaking down often, forcing him to get a newer model, which increased his debt. His job didn't earn enough to pay for all of his monthly obligations, so he needed to dip into this savings. On the flip side, the new job at Bank of America allowed him to invest a small amount of his pay in a 401(k) plan.

Daniel's Career and Financial Plan: Part 4 (August 2010–May 2013)

★ New job increases income; contributes 12 percent of each paycheck to retirement savings.

★ Outside investments have grown to $30,000.

★ Mortgage loan modified, reducing monthly payments.

★ New marriage will provide more family income.

At this point, Daniel is only two years removed from separating from military service. He has achieved some of his career and financial goals, but he isn't yet earning a strong income and has also suffered some personal setbacks. Fortunately, a new opportunity came along, and he accepted a job in mid-2010 with an organization that is now part of ClearPoint. A higher starting salary and pay raises during the first three years on the job have helped him increase his income. The pay increase has allowed him to contribute 12 percent of his gross income to his retirement savings plan.

To save money on his mortgage payment, Daniel's mortgage company modified his mortgage loan, dropping the payment to $550 each month. Meanwhile, an increase in the stock market has helped increase the value of his outside investments. Finally, he has decided to remarry. He and his future wife believe a two-income family will give them more financial flexibility.

What Have We Learned From Daniel's Story?

We know writing down our goals, developing a plan to achieve them, and executing that plan are not easy things to do. But if you're going to get anywhere, you need to take these steps. By completing his college degree, Daniel was able to eventually get on a management track that has set up his career path for many years to come.

Sometimes you need a little bit of luck to achieve some goals. In Daniel's case, his military service helped him find a high-paying contract job overseas when little work was available in the United States. This job allowed him to begin implementing a long-term financial plan to save for his own retirement and his son's college education. But it also came with a price, the divorce.

The toughest part of fulfilling a long-term goal is overcoming the obstacles along the way. Many unexpected events can change the course of our lives and cause short-term pain to our finances. These changes include a wide range of life events: job layoffs, marriage or divorce, a new child in your family, large medical expenses, and even unexpected repairs to your home or car. And so, during the course of saving money for your long-term goal, you may need to make some adjustments.

On the other hand, any success you achieve at work may help accelerate your ability to attain a long-term goal. A promotion at work includes a pay raise, bonus and stock options, or a large tax refund that can be applied toward the savings to meet your goal.

Savings and Investment Strategies Checklist

The right tools are critical to helping you achieve your goals. Use this checklist as you research various savings and investment tools. Identify strategies you might be interested in and record important notes for each. Contact a financial advisor for assistance or to learn more.

✓	Savings and Money Management Accounts	
	Interest bearing checking account	Notes:
	Interest bearing savings account	Notes:

	Certificates of deposit	Notes:
	U.S. savings bonds	Notes:
	Money market account	Notes:
	Other:	Notes:
✓	Investment Accounts	
	401(k)	Notes:
	403(b)	Notes:
	Individual Retirement Account (IRA)	Notes:

	Roth IRA	Notes:
	Pension	Notes:
	Annuity	Notes:
	Stocks	Notes:
	Mutual fund	Notes:
	myRA	Notes:
✓	College Savings Accounts	
	529 savings plan	Notes:

	529 prepaid plan	Notes:
	Individual Development Account (IDA)	Notes:
	Other:	Notes:

8

How to Reshape Damaged Credit

For millions of Americans, the most important number in their financial lives is their credit score. This is because their credit has been damaged by past mistakes—loans they've been unable to pay, large amounts owed on several credit cards, and even bankruptcy. Once this happens, it can be difficult—but certainly not impossible—to dig yourself out of this hole.

We know that it's easy for young service members to make credit mistakes. In the spring of 2013, credit counselor Rachelle George of ClearPoint spoke with a 19-year-old active duty service member who had defaulted on several bills—her cell phone, utilities, and credit cards. George says young service members are often the target of sales representatives because of their stable pay. "There are laws against offering credit cards to college students until they are 21, but there is no law stopping credit card companies from selling products to young service members," George says.

The problem with bad credit is that it doesn't end with lenders. Though it may seem unreasonable, many potential employers will ask to check your credit report. An estimated 47 percent of U.S. employers conducted credit background checks on job candidates, according to a 2012 survey by the Society for Human Resource Management.

For people with damaged credit, it's important to know what you need to do to get back on track. You need to understand how to read a credit report, how it affects your financial life, and what steps you can take to improve it.

Credit Reports and Credit Scores

Let's start by understanding credit reports.

Equifax, TransUnion, and Experian are the three companies that produce credit reports on every person in the United States that has credit. All three collect and maintain a history of your credit activity, such as credit cards, mortgages, and other loans. This information is reported to them by lenders and creditors with whom you have accounts. The three credit bureaus also collect other information, such as bankruptcies, civil judgments, liens, and any debt owed to collection companies. All of this information is listed on your credit report.

Don't Pay to Get Your Credit Report!

Even if you've been overseas for years, you are probably familiar with the Website FreeCreditScore.com. Television commercials have been broadcast continuously since 2007 featuring members of a fictitious rock band that experience credit problems as they try to make it in the music world. The commercials pitch FreeCreditScore.com as the place to go to get your credit back in shape.

FreeCreditScore.com and FreeCreditReport.com are owned by Experian. But don't go to these Websites for a copy of your credit report. Instead, anyone can obtain a free copy of their credit report at *www.annualcreditreport.com*. Federal law requires each of the three credit bureaus to provide anyone a free credit report once per year, which means that you can get three free credit reports annually.

Reading a Credit Report

Once you have your credit report, review it carefully for any errors. If there are errors, you can get them corrected, which may reflect positively your credit score. Some of the typical errors on a credit report include:

★ Incorrect personal information. A friend of mine that cosigned a car loan with his daughter recently noticed two of his daughter's past home addresses on his credit report. Even though he has lived in his current home for 21 years, the errors could lead a potential lender or employer to believe he has moved frequently in recent years. This could give the impression that he is unstable and needed to move, or that he has multiple residences.

★ Accounts that are someone else's. This often happens to people with a common last name, such as Smith or Jones. And it could mean that a negative credit problem that belongs to someone else has ended up on your report.

★ Items known as negative items, such as bankruptcy, that are more than seven years old.

★ An unauthorized "hard" inquiry. This is when a lender or other organization pulls your credit history without your permission when someone is trying to obtain credit under your name.

Disputing Errors on Your Credit Report

Contact one of the credit bureaus to dispute any incorrect information, as well as the organization that provided the information to the credit bureau. Both are responsible for correcting inaccurate or incomplete information under a federal law called the Fair Credit Reporting Act.

You will need to send a written statement, along with copies of documents that support your position. Ask the credit bureaus and the creditors to send a notice of correction to potential lenders and employers. Once you have submitted your written statement, the credit bureau must investigate the items in question within 30 days.

In addition to providing your complete name and address, your letter should clearly identify each item that you are disputing; state the facts and explain why you are disputing the information and request a deletion or correction. Here is a sample letter:

Date

Credit Reporting Agency Name

Credit Reporting Agency Address

RE: **(disputed item)/(credit report confirmation number)**

Dear **(Credit Reporting Agency Name)**,

    I am writing this letter to dispute the following items in my credit report. I have enclosed a copy of the credit report I received from your agency, with the disputed items circled.

    (List name, account number, and type of item disputed) is inaccurate because **(list a detailed explanation of the item and why you are disputing it)**. Please **(remove, update, correct)** this item to reflect the most accurate information.

    In addition to the above mentioned credit report, I have enclosed **(list a description of any enclosed documentation to support your dispute, if applicable)** to support my dispute. I am requesting that you investigate this/these disputed item(s) and **(remove, update, correct)** it/them as soon as possible.

    Your prompt attention to this matter is most appreciated.

Sincerely,

(signature)

Your Name

Your Address

Enclosures: **(list of documents enclosed)**

Finally, you can go to the credit bureau's Website and add a 100-word statement to your credit report, which lets potential lenders and employers see that it has inaccurate information. You can also utilize this statement to explain a potential hardship which caused you to miss payments on certain bills during a specific period.

What Is a Credit Score?

All of the information in your credit report determines your credit score. The purpose of a credit score is to predict risk if a lender provides you with credit. In effect, the lender wants to know that you will repay the money they are loaning you.

The most recognized credit score is the FICO score, which was developed by FICO (originally called Fair Isaac Company), a company based in San Jose, California. According to myFICO.com, the FICO score is used in more than 90 percent of all lending decisions. The FICO score ranges from 300 to 850. The higher your credit score, the better credit risk you are to any lender. The FICO score is made up of five different categories.

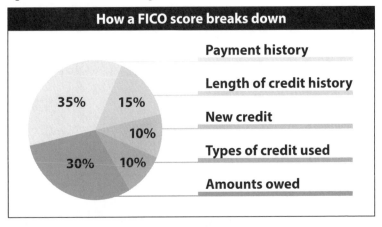

As you can see, the amount of money you owe and your payment history make up roughly two-thirds of your credit score. According to myFICO.com, late payments will lower your FICO score, but establishing or re-establishing a good track record of making payments on time will raise your score.

Although you can obtain your credit report for free, my-FICO.com charges $19.95 to get a copy of your credit score, though customers of Discover and Barclaycard US provide free FICO scores directly to their card holders. However, you can get an idea of your score by tapping into other services.

For example, CreditKarma.com provides users with a proprietary credit score generated from TransUnion's TransRisk score model. Credit Karma's score model ranges from 300 to 850, which is the same scale as the FICO score, but the mathematical algorithm used to calculate the score is different.

What Is a Bad Credit Score?

The credit score used to define a person with a subprime credit rating varies with the lender and loan. A good rule of thumb is that a person is considered to have subprime credit if his or her score is around 620 or lower. For example, Equifax considers a credit score below 620 to fall into the subprime category and says the low score generally prevents a consumer from getting favorable interest rates on a range of financial services, from credit cards to car loans and mortgages.

Many lenders will likely consider anyone with a score between 600 and 650 to be a high credit risk.

Advice for Building Credit

FICO recommends that the best advice for building credit is to manage it responsibly over time instead of attempting any quick fix. It says the best way to do that is to check your credit report, set up payment reminders, and reduce the amount of money you owe.

Because payment history accounts for 35 percent of your credit score, let's focus on some actions you can take to improve this category. FICO has these tips:

★ "Pay your bills on time." Any late payments can have a negative effect on your FICO score.

★ "If you have missed payments, get current and stay current. The longer you pay your bills on time after being late, the more your FICO score should increase."

★ If you are having problems paying your bills, my-FICO.com recommends that you contact your creditors or see a credit counselor. It says that getting help from a credit counseling service will not damage your credit score.

Tips about the "Amounts Owed" Category

According to FICO, this category can be easier to clean up than your payment history—the other big category that makes up a FICO score. Here is their advice on how to achieve that goal:

★ "Keep balances low on credit cards and other 'revolving credit.'" This means that if you have a credit card with a $1,000 limit, the balance cannot always be around $800 or $900 if you want to increase your score over time.

★ "Pay off debt rather than moving it around." FICO says the most effective way to improve your credit score in this category is to pay down your credit cards. Interestingly, it says that owing the same amount on fewer credit cards may lower your score.

★ "Don't close unused credit cards as a short-term strategy to raise your score."

★ "Don't open a number of new credit cards that you don't need, just to increase your available credit."

(Source: *www.myfico.com/crediteducation/improveyourscore. aspx.*)

Implement Positive Behavior

The good news is that just about anyone can rebuild his or her credit, no matter how damaged it is. For example, badly in debt and late with her bills, Melesia Lobban decided it was time for a change. After getting help from a credit counselor, she created a budget, paid off her overdue bills, and started saving for a home.

According to the *Orlando Sentinel*, Melesia's credit score soared more than 50 points, to 660, which could help her save thousands of dollars by landing a better interest rate when she applies for a mortgage.

"It was really an eye-opening experience," said Lobban, a certified nursing assistant who lives in Casselberry, Florida, about her climb out of debt and the effect on her credit. "I saved money on food and gas, [then] I saved money on late fees, because I could pay the bills on time. And now I've saved enough for a down payment—all I need to do is find a house that's affordable for me."

Now you know what to do to get back on track. Once you obtain your credit report, dispute any inaccurate information and understand what it takes to raise your credit score. Also, make sure to obtain and review your credit report at least every four months. A thorough check of your credit report at least once a year can also help you prevent identity theft and fraud, as well as address any problems before they get out of control.

If you make timely and consistent payments, keep credit card balances low, and stick to your priority spending plan, I know you will be successful.

Negotiating With Creditors

No matter what we do, an unforeseen event can be the cause of financial problems. In this day and age, it's common to lose a job, experience costly medical bills, or have a life-changing event, such as a new baby or a divorce.

If you are in danger of falling behind on any payments, you need to take action to minimize the damage to your credit. As hard as it may be, I recommend that you contact your creditors while your accounts are still current to discuss alternative payment arrangements. In some cases, you could be eligible for hardship programs or another plan that will keep your accounts current for some time.

There are several risks to falling behind on your payments, including increased interest rates, as well as late and over-limit fees. And any account that becomes delinquent will have an impact on your credit report and score. Finally, if a creditor tries to contact you and they are unsuccessful, they may sell your account to a collection agency, charge it off, or begin legal proceedings. Once this happens, you will likely lose the opportunity to negotiate a new payment plan.

Before making a call to your creditors, review your current spending plan and evaluate your situation. Try to answer the following questions:

★ How much can you afford to pay to each of your creditors every month?

★ When can you expect your financial situation to improve?

★ When can you resume regular monthly payments?

★ Do you have any savings? Are you expecting a tax refund or other lump sum that can be used to pay off your debts?

★ What type of debt do you have and who are your creditors? For example, do you have a mortgage loan, car loan, and credit card debt?

Tips for Effective Negotiation

Once you understand your financial situation, contact your creditors to negotiate a possible alternative payment plan. Here are some tips to use in speaking with creditors:

★ **Know your best offer.** This is the amount you can afford to pay each month. Don't agree to an amount if you can't make the payments. When negotiating, know your best offer and stick to it.

★ **Have realistic expectations.** Allow some room for compromise, but be realistic and avoid making promises you can't keep. It will only derail your negotiation and could further hurt your financial situation.

★ **Talk to the right person.** Ask for the "hardship" department or request to speak with a manager or supervisor. It may be helpful to make the following statement: "I'm having a financial hardship that is preventing me from making payments. Are you the right person who can help me with an alternative payment arrangement?" If you get transferred to the collections department by mistake, hang up and try again.

★ **Be direct.** Once you have reached a person who is empowered to help you, be prepared to make an offer for payment. This information should include how much money you can pay and when you expect to resume regular payments.

★ **Keep accurate records.** Keep records of conversations with creditors. This should include the date, name of the person you spoke with, their contact information or department, and the outcome of the conversation.

★ **Put agreements in writing.** Once you've reached an agreement, get it in writing and send a letter to the creditor recapping the agreement. Include your name, address, and account number on all correspondence. Send all written communications by certified mail, return receipt requested.

★ **Maintain regular contact.** If your situation changes and you're unable to fulfill your new payment obligations, notify them immediately.

Possible Solutions

Credit counselors can sometimes help people find a solution simply by helping them develop a budget and reducing their expenses. Here's a great example.

ClearPoint counselor Kevin Weekley helped a military service member who owed $22,000 in student loans and was delinquent on his payments. The service member was concerned that the collection agency would attempt to have his wages garnished, which would endanger his security clearance.

Weekley worked with the service member to reduce his spending on many non-essential items, giving him a monthly budget surplus of $277. With his budget in place, Weekley held a conference call with the service member and the collection agency, which agreed to put him on a payment plan of $275 a month for nine months. If the service member agreed to make payments for nine consecutive months, the loan would be transferred back to the original lender and his wages would not be garnished. As you can imagine, the service member was extremely pleased with this outcome.

No two situations are alike, so creditors have a variety of options. Here are some of the most common solutions:

★ Monthly payments for less money than the original minimum payment required. But a reduced payment plan may only be offered temporarily.

★ Deferred payments. This means that no payment is required for a certain amount of time. However, the amount of the deferred payments will likely be added to the end of the loan and additional fees or interest may be applied to the original loan amount.

★ A reduction in interest and fees. This option could be offered temporarily or over the life of the loan.

Additional Questions to Ask Creditors

Once you reach a solution with one or more creditors, you need to know how the agreement will affect other parts of your financial life. Although most people are often happy to receive any offer from a creditor, you need to understand all of the consequences of any agreement.

Be sure to ask the following questions:

★ How will my new payment plan be reported to the credit bureaus? Make sure that a creditor is not reporting a reduced payment as one that is now delinquent.

★ When will I be expected to resume regular monthly payments?

★ What happens if I can't fulfill the terms of this arrangement?

★ Will there be additional fees or penalties assessed as a result of this arrangement?

The Collection Process

As you are attempting to negotiate an alternative payment, one or more creditors may turn your account over to a collection agency. Once your account is past due, it could be sold to a third-party debt collector that will attempt to collect the money you owe. If this happens, the original creditor may no longer communicate with you about that debt. You could be contacted by a collection agency, an attorney collecting a debt or one representing a collection agency, or an independent collection business.

Collection companies often pay a percentage of the amount owed on the account to the original creditor, then attempt to collect the debt from you. The goal of the collection agency is to make as much money as possible. But they must follow specific guidelines when dealing with any individual.

Restrictions on Collection Agencies

According to the Fair Debt Collection Practices Act, a collector can contact you at home by telephone, mail, e-mail, fax, or telegram. They can discuss the debt with you, your spouse, or attorney and they can contact your friends, family, and neighbors to locate you. Collectors must send you a validation notice within five days of their first contact about the debt. The notice tells you how much you owe, the name of the creditor, and what to do if you are disputing the debt.

However, debt collectors cannot take these actions:

★ They cannot call you before 8 a.m. or after 9 p.m. They cannot discuss the debt with friends, family members, or neighbors.

★ If you write a letter to the debt collector asking them not to contact you at home, they must stop.

★ If you or your employer verbally asks them to stop contacting you at work, they must stop.

★ They cannot make false statements, give false information, or use harsh or threatening language.

★ They are prohibited from depositing a post-dated check early, collecting more than you owe, or threatening to take your property. To learn more about these restrictions according to federal law, visit *www.ftc.gov.*

Despite all of these protections, you are still legally responsible for paying any debt and could be sued by the debt collector or the original creditor.

Protect Your Rights

If you believe your rights have been violated by a debt collector, you may want to contact an attorney for legal advice. You may also consider contacting your state attorney, the Consumer Financial Protection Bureau, the Federal Trade Commission, and the Better Business Bureau.

If you decide to take action, you can sue the debt collector within one year of the violation. If you win, you could be compensated for costs you incurred. Even if you can't prove the exact costs, you could still be awarded up to $1,000 by a court if you win.

Wage Garnishments and Judgments

If a person is behind in their payments, and a creditor does not believe that they will be able to collect the debt, the creditor can file a lawsuit asking for a judgment for the amount that is owed.

If the creditor is successful, the court will order that wages be deducted from a person's paycheck or liens be issued against their property to collect the debt. This action is called a wage garnishment.

Garnishments can occur on any debt in default. In addition to credit card debt, delinquent taxes and child support payments are subject to judgments. State and federal laws determine how much money can be taken from a person's paycheck. In most cases, a creditor can garnish 10 percent of your gross income. For more information, visit *www.dol.gov* and view the Employment Law Guide.

If a person is unemployed, the court could issue a judgment garnishing a person's bank accounts. Or they could issue a property lien, which means that when a property is sold, money from the sale of the property is used to pay the debt.

Laws protect some income from garnishments, such as social security, disability, and veteran's payments. To learn more, visit *www.dol.gov* and select "wages."

Are You at Risk?

Most judgments and wage garnishments can be avoided by addressing your financial situation as soon as possible. Before you default on your debt, here are some steps to consider:

* ★ Contact your creditors immediately. As soon as you know you can't make your regular payments, discuss your situation with creditors and explore possible alternative payment arrangements.

* ★ Respond to collection calls. Avoiding calls or letters from collectors could lead to third-party collection agencies or legal action.

* ★ Consider credit counseling. Contact a nonprofit credit counseling organization to discuss your options. As I've discussed in previous chapters, most of these organizations offer a debt repayment plan that may enable you to reduce interest rates on credit cards and thus afford your payments. To find a nonprofit credit counseling organization, visit *www.nfcc.org*.

★ Contact an attorney. If a judgment, wage garnishment, or any other legal action has been threatened, contact an attorney to discuss your options.

What If a Judgment or Wage Garnishment Is Issued?

If a judgment has been issued against you, don't panic. Although the situation looks bleak, you still have some options to get control your financial situation. For example:

★ Participate in all court hearings. It's important to attend all court hearings to defend yourself and fully understand the situation. Consider seeking legal advice for help.

★ Understand garnishment laws and restrictions. These laws vary for each state, and state laws differ from the federal government. The amount of any garnishment must be for the lowest amount set by a state and the federal guidelines. To learn more about the federal law, visit *www.dol.gov* and select "compliance." To learn more about state laws, visit *www.dol.gov* and select your state.

★ Request the amount of the garnishment be lowered. If the amount of a garnishment affects your ability to support yourself and your family, you may ask the court to lower the amount of the garnishment.

Creditor Negotiation Worksheet

Use this worksheet when negotiating payment alternatives with your creditors. First, evaluate your financial situation. Then, for each creditor, list current payment details, how much you can afford to pay each month, how long you need reduced payments, whether settlement is an option and, if so, the amount you can afford.

Evaluate Your Financial Situation		
What situation caused you to fall behind on your payments?		
When do you expect your financial situation to improve?		
Do you have money set aside/are you expecting a lump sum of money?		
Amount: $		
Source:		
Date available:		
Creditor Information	**Proposed Payments**	**Proposed Settlement**
Mortgage Phone: Current APR: Payment: $	$ □ 1–12 months □ 12 months +	□ No □ Yes $
Automobile Phone: Current APR: Payment: $	$ □ 1–12 months □ 12 months +	□ No □ Yes $

Student Loan	$	□ No
Phone:	□ 1–12 months	□ Yes
Current APR:	□ 12 months +	$
Payment: $		
Credit Card	$	□ No
Phone:	□ 1–12 months	□ Yes
Current APR:	□ 12 months +	$
Payment: $		
Other	$	□ No
Phone:	□ 1–12 months	□ Yes
Current APR:	□ 12 months +	$
Payment: $		

9

How to Avoid Financial Scams

Plenty of organizations try to sell products that appeal to veterans. And some of these organizations aren't on the up-and-up. Even the President of the United States says there are people trying to pick your pocket.

In June 2012, President Barack Obama told active duty service members at Fort Stewart, near Savannah, Georgia, that some for-profit colleges and technical colleges go after military men and women "just for the money." In his speech, the President was blunt. "They don't care about you," he said. "They care about your cash. That's appalling, that's disgraceful. They're trying to swindle and hoodwink you."

Following complaints against some of these organizations, the President signed a broad order in mid-2012 that partially addressed fraudulent marketing and recruiting practices aimed at military families eligible for federal education aid under the GI Bill. According to the Associated Press, the new protections make it harder for postsecondary and technical schools to misrepresent themselves to military students.

That same month, the *New York Times* reported that attorneys general in 20 states announced a settlement with QuinStreet Inc., an online marketing company, forcing QuinStreet to turn over the Web address *www.gibill.com* to the Department of Veterans Affairs and pay $2.5 million to the states. The attorneys general claimed QuinStreet used "false, deceptive and misleading representations" that had the potential to deceive users into believing that the Website was endorsed by the federal government.

By December 2012, the Veterans Administration owned the trademark for "GI Bill." However, trademark protection is not permanently guaranteed and the VA must actively police the trademark and pursue anyone who infringes on it or the protection can expire. In June 2013, several U.S. senators introduced a bill to permanently protect the phrase "GI Bill" from abuse.

Guarding Against Financial Scams

Financial scams are so prevalent today that they are a part of everyday life. Be aware that the words "veterans" or "military families" in an organization's name, or an ad, doesn't necessarily mean that the organization is there to serve veterans or the families of active-duty personnel.

In the old days, the scam artists were easier to spot. Today, they are often people with a sophisticated knowledge of banking and investments who know how to mask their true intentions.

In addition, many offers for help are perfectly legal. As we discussed earlier, firms that offer to modify your mortgage loan, or those that offer to settle your debt or repair your credit, are often operating within the law. The problem is that they either can't deliver on their offer or that you can receive the same services for free or for little cost from other organizations. And sometimes you can even do these things yourself.

Many of these offers seem perfectly legitimate—until you have paid your money and not received the services or benefits promised. In this chapter, I would like to give you tips and information about how to avoid the bad actors, understand which organizations to trust, and point you to reliable Websites and other sources of information.

Be Smart: Always Protect Your Personal and Financial Information

We would never strike up a conversation with a friend or coworker and offer to tell them our Social Security number, the number of our bank checking account, or the personal code to our debit card. But some people are tempted to give away this information when they receive an offer through the Internet or the mail that promises a gift or a prize. And it can be even more intriguing if the offer insists that you must act immediately to claim any prize, whether it's a $1,000 gift card or a free weekend at the beach.

These are the easy offers to ignore. Don't ever be sucked into giving away your Social Security number or private financial information to any organization, telephone caller, or

Website in return for a gift or other prize. You can bet that these people want access to this information to get into your pocket and steal your money.

Identity Theft Is the Number One Scam

More than 12.6 million Americans were victims of identity theft in 2012, up by one million from 2011. Each year, the Federal Trade Commission (FTC) takes complaints from consumers nationwide about various types of fraud. And every year, identity theft tops the list of complaints.

In 2012, the FTC received more than two million complaints and 18 percent—nearly one in five—were related to identity theft. Among the identity theft complaints, the government agency cited a sharp rise in reports of tax return refund hijacking. Of the nearly 370,000 identity theft complaints, more than 43 percent were tax- or wage-related fraud.

After the FTC's most recent report was released in 2013, NBC News reported that there are three basic types of identity theft related to taxes and wages. Here they are:

★ The most common is when the scammer, using your Social Security number, applies for an income tax refund in your name. If the crook gets your refund before you file your return, it can hold up the process for months.

★ Identity thieves sometimes misuse Social Security numbers to create bogus dependents to boost their fraudulent refund. Again, this delays legitimate refunds.

★ The crooks also use stolen Social Security numbers to get a job. Victims don't find out about this until they get a notice from the IRS that says they're underreporting their income.

According to the *Atlanta Journal-Constitution*, Atlanta police arrested Erkes Antwon Green in February 2013 on a charge of bank fraud, alleging that he opened a bank account online using a stolen identity, depositing a stolen check for $46,000, and later trying to make an ATM withdrawal. Police later discovered 142 files in Green's apartment that had names, birthdays, and Social Security numbers, leading them to believe he was filing tax returns for all 142 people.

Law enforcement officials believe Green is part of a network of identity thieves who have stolen personal information from hundreds of people by using something known as a "keystroke grabber"—technology that siphons information from a person's personal accounts, but can go undetected for months.

Steps to Protect Your Identity

★ There are several actions you can take to protect your identity. Some of these recommendations may seem like an overreaction, but with identity theft continuing to mount, I want you to know how you can protect yourself.

★ First, examine every possible way to protect your personal information. When conducting business online or over the phone, never share personal or financial information unless you have initiated contact and know who you are talking to.

Internet Safety Tips

Millions of people use the Internet every day to let friends, family, work colleagues, and others know their whereabouts 24/7. But putting too much information online about your personal business can be risky. So here are some recommendations on ways to limit your communications that will help protect your identity and personal information:

★   Make certain that you restrict the information you share. Review your online settings on Facebook, LinkedIn, and other social networks and limit personal information that, if stolen, could cause harm.

★   Do not post travel plans online as this information only alerts identity thieves about your absence from your home. Wait until you are securely back home before sharing information and photos of vacations and out-of-town trips.

★   Choose your "friends" carefully. Don't subscribe to the "more is better" theory when it comes to social networks. Keeping your circle of friends small will significantly reduce your risk.

★   These days, even young children are online regularly, so monitor their activity and make certain that they are following the same guidelines. We know that many adults online pose as children, so it's up to us to make certain our children are not giving away critical personal information.

More Internet Safety Tips

Here are some other Internet safety tips related specifically to e-mail, online shopping, and virus protection:

★ Ignore e-mails with links that want you to "verify" personal information. Do not respond to these e-mails even if they appear to be from your bank or financial institution. Instead, go directly to the bank's Website by typing in their URL into a new browser window; log into your account to make any necessary updates or inquiries about your account.

★ Instead of using your debit card when shopping online, use a credit card or secure third party payment tool like PayPal. This will provide you with an extra layer of protection from online identity thieves. In addition, look for an icon of a lock in the URL section of the Website as well as HTTPS// at the beginning of the Web address.

★ Make certain to run some type of virus and malware protection software on your computer, and ensure it is set to scan your system automatically once a week. Also, keep important files in a secure cloud environment in case of theft. Finally, install a firewall for additional protection.

Empty Your Wallet

Our wallets and purses contain much of our vital personal financial information. To limit any damage that can occur if your wallet is lost or stolen, I want you to empty your wallet and take out the credit cards that you don't use regularly. I also advise against carrying your Social Security card and other cards that may contain your Social Security number, such as insurance cards. Once you minimize the information you keep in your wallet, copy both sides of all cards and keep them in a secure location.

In addition, never carry your checkbook. If someone steals your checkbook and writes fraudulent checks; there could be a warrant issued for your arrest. If you're wondering how that could happen, let me give you a possible scenario.

A woman loses her purse that has her identification, credit cards, and checkbook. A thief creates a new identity utilizing the woman's name and personal information. The thief writes checks using the new identification, but with a photo of the thief.

If these bad checks are turned over to the district attorney's office, the victim could be summoned to court. And if that person doesn't appear in court, a warrant will be issued for their arrest. To avoid this form of identity theft, write checks at home and go to the post office to mail them. Here are some other tips:

★ If you still use paper checks to pay bills, never print your Social Security number on your checks. When you order checks, receive these items at your bank instead of your home.

★ Clean out your car and remove receipts and anything else containing personal information.

★ Clear Social Security numbers from public records. Check any online records with your local Clerk of Courts. If you have bought a home in the past, your records are there and your Social Security number could be visible. Make a request that this information be concealed in online copies of your records. Many of the Clerk of Courts' offices actively ensure this information is hidden, but older public records may still be in need of this update. This also applies if you have placed a copy of your DD-214 on file with the court; ensure your serial number has been redacted from this public document.

★ When sending postal mail, I recommend that you make a trip to the post office or a U.S. mailbox. Four years ago, I redesigned my home mailbox and specifically took off the red flag because I never use it to send mail. Raising the red flag lets thieves know that I may be paying a bill with a personal check that has my name, address, and bank account information. Instead, I utilize my bank's secure bill pay system and I take any other personal checks that I may write to my local post office for drop off or utilize the mailroom at my employer.

★ When it comes to shredding documents, don't take chances. Make certain that you destroy everything, including applications for credit cards, other loan products, and credit card receipts. Shred any piece of paper that has your personal information on it.

Burn Old Papers

Every fall, my mother and I celebrate "burn day." For an entire year we collect old receipts, past bills, old checking account books, past deposit slips, and other items which include our name and address. We collect and package all of this paper, place it in containers, and wait for burn day.

On this day, we go into my mom's backyard with the container. We empty all of our information into the container and let the fire free us from worries of identity thieves tracking our information. For our most recent burn day, my mother collected three large trash bags filled with pre-approved applications for credit cards, along with miscellaneous bills and notices from the doctor. I had two large bags with the same items, including a box of bank checks that were never used when I closed an account.

Consider Setting up Fraud Alerts on Your Credit Report

Credit reports are another place where identity theft can be detected. Placing a fraud alert on your credit report tells lenders and creditors that they must always verify your identification by contacting you before extending a credit line or loan in your name. This can help protect your identity from fraud by preventing a thief from opening any new accounts in your name.

There are three types of fraud alerts:

1. **Initial Fraud Alert.** If you're concerned about identity theft, but haven't yet become a victim,

this fraud alert will protect your credit from un-verified access for at least 90 days.

2. **Extended Fraud Alert.** For victims of identity theft, an extended fraud alert will protect your credit for seven years.

3. **Active Duty Military Alert.** For those in the military who want to protect their credit while deployed, this type of fraud alert will last for one year.

Once you've placed a fraud alert on your credit, you can remove it at any time. In order to initiate a fraud alert, contact one of the three credit bureaus; that bureau will be required to notify the other two credit bureaus to place an alert on your file. Here's how to contact each of the credit bureaus:

★ **Equifax:** *www.equifax.com* or by calling 1-800-525-6285.

★ **Experian:** *www.experian.com* or by calling 1-888-397-3742.

★ **TransUnion:** *www.transunion.com* or by calling 1-800-680-7289.

Although fraud alerts won't prevent an identity thief from using accounts you already have, they can help prevent them from opening any more accounts in your name. An initial fraud alert, which stays on your credit report for at least 90 days, is a good idea if you suspect you have been a victim of identity theft. It is a great step to take if your wallet has been stolen, or if you think you may have been scammed by a telephone or Internet marketer and have given out personal information. When you place an initial fraud alert on your credit report, potential creditors must use what the law refers to as "reasonable policies and procedures" to verify your identity before issuing credit in your name.

If you are the victim of identity theft, you can place an extended fraud alert on your credit report for seven years. A formal complaint report must be submitted to place the alert and, once placed, creditors must contact you or meet with you in person before they issue you credit.

Fraud alerts can be removed from your credit report at your request with appropriate documentation. Keep in mind that though a fraud alert can protect you from further damage from identity thieves, there may also be delays in your legitimate attempts to obtain credit. Keep information current, and consider including a cell phone number for quick access.

Freezing Your Credit

A credit freeze can protect you from the vast majority of identity theft that involves opening a new line of credit. The freeze is permanent and once placed, potential creditors and other third parties will not be able to get access to your credit report unless you temporarily lift the freeze, making it unlikely that an identity thief would be able to open a new account in your name.

Placing a credit freeze does not affect your credit score—nor does it keep you from getting your free annual credit report, or from buying your credit report or score. In most states, there is no fee for identity theft victims to place a freeze. In other cases, there may be a fee to place the freeze, lift it temporarily, or remove it altogether. For more information on fees for your state, check this Website: *http://www. consumersunion.org/campaigns/learn_more/003484indiv. html*. Placing a credit freeze requires that you contact each of the reporting bureaus individually.

If you haven't been a victim of identity theft, should you freeze your credit? My answer here is that it depends on the situation. I, and several of my colleagues at work, have frozen our credit. I do it because I already have a house, a car that is paid off, and a couple of credit cards.

I'm not in the market to buy anything new and it doesn't make sense for my credit to be exposed for possible theft. Freezing my credit is not difficult to do and it's a great tool to keep my spending in check. For example, when I visit a furniture store and consider spending $2,000, and the store offers me no interest for two years, I decline. I know that I can't get credit until I pay each of the three credit bureaus to temporarily lift the freeze on my credit report. If I really want that furniture, I'll come back and get it when I have cash.

What if You Have a History of Identity Theft?

If you've had an identity theft problem and feel you may need the services of a private company, you may want to consider subscribing to an identity theft protection service. Prices for these services range from about $100 to $250 annually and they provide such services as placing and renewing fraud alerts on your credit reports, requesting removal of your address from junk mail lists and pre-approved credit card mailings, ordering your free credit reports on your behalf, contacting creditors in the event of a lost or stolen wallet, and providing resources to help you if you are the victim of identity theft while a member of their service.

Do you really need to pay for credit monitoring or identity theft protection? I don't endorse any credit monitoring or identity theft protection service. You can take all the same steps provided by these services on your own. If you do opt to sign up for a service, understand the specific terms of coverage and the limitations of each policy.

If You Are a Victim of Identity Theft, What Should You Do?

If you are victimized by identity theft, take the following steps:

★ Contact your local police department, file a report, and get a copy. Make additional copies of the police report because you may need to submit proof to creditors about the theft.

★ Place a fraud alert on your credit file by contacting the fraud departments of any of the three major credit bureaus. Here is the contact information for these organizations:

• Experian: 1-888-EXPERIAN (397-3742); *www.experian.com*; P.O. Box 9532, Allen, TX 75013.

• TransUnion: 1-800-680-7289; *www.transunion.com*; Fraud Victim Assistance

Division, P.O. Box 6790, Fullerton, CA 92834-6790.

- Equifax: 1-800-525-6285; *www.equifax.com*; P.O. Box 740256, Atlanta, GA 30374.

You only need to contact one credit bureau because each is required to contact the other two. Once the fraud alert is placed, each credit bureau must also provide you with a free copy of your credit report. Have them limit any extraneous personal information if they are sending your report by mail. Review the reports and look for inquiries or open accounts from companies you don't know and debts you can't explain.

★ If you believe an account is fraudulent, close it. I also recommend that you contact the security or fraud department of each company to discuss this account. Keep records from each conversation, including dates, times, and the person who provided the information. Also, write down what additional action is needed and when so that you can follow-up regularly and check the status. If you send any correspondence, make a copy of it first for your records and send it by certified mail, return receipt requested.

★ When accessing old accounts online or opening a new account, always use new creative passwords and personal identification numbers (PINs) that you haven't used in the past. Do not use passwords that could be easy to guess such as your birthday, telephone number, child's name, and your mother's maiden name.

★   Once you clear up your credit report, check them periodically to make sure no new activity has occurred.

★   I also recommend filing a complaint with the Federal Trade Commission. This action can help law enforcement officials find and arrest identity thieves. The FTC's online complaint form is at *www.ftccomplaintassistant.gov.* You can also call their toll-free Identity Theft Hotline at 1-877-ID-THEFT (438-4338).

Identity Theft Checklist

Follow the guide below to identify and record actions you should take if you suspect you are the victim of identity theft.

Action	Date
Contact one of the three credit-reporting agencies (Equifax, Experian, and TransUnion). That agency will notify the others. A "fraud alert" will be automatically placed on each of your credit reports within 24 hours.	
Once the credit-reporting agencies are notified, you'll automatically receive a free credit report from each of the three agencies, and you will be opted out of pre-approved credit card and insurance offers.	
Contact creditors for any accounts that have been tampered with or opened without your knowledge. Be sure to put your complaints in writing.	
Contact the FTC at 877-438-4338. Fill out the Identity Theft Affidavit at the FTC's Website, make copies, and send to creditors.	

Alert the police. Make sure the police report lists all fraud accounts. Give as much documented information as possible. Get a copy of the report and send it to the creditors and the credit-reporting agencies as proof of the crime.	
Change all your account passwords.	
Notify the Office of the Inspector General if your Social Security number has been fraudulently used. Call 800-269-0271.	
You may need to change your driver's license number if someone is using yours as an ID. Go to the Department of Motor Vehicles to get a new number.	
Other:	
Other:	

10

Protecting Your Investments: Understanding Insurance

Insurance is the last piece in building your budget and beginning to develop an overall financial plan. Whether buying a house or a car, or needing to protect your family with life insurance, it is necessary to build the cost of insuring these assets into our budgets.

I recommend that you carry insurance to cover your health, auto, life, and home. You also need to protect your income in the event of a disability and older veterans may also want to invest in long-term care insurance. In this chapter, I want to provide you with a basic understanding of how insurance works, how to buy it, and how to file a claim.

What Is the Purpose of Insurance?

There are a lot of simple questions about insurance, but often, the answers aren't as simple. So let's start out with a basic understanding of insurance.

Insurance is a safeguard to protect you against the financial impact of an accident or catastrophic event. It is not meant to cover the costs of small, unexpected events or to replace parts of items due to regular wear and tear.

One of the most common events where insurance protects us is a severe car accident. If a person is injured in a car accident, medical insurance will pay the doctor and hospital bills. If a person is forced to miss work because of his or her injuries, disability insurance ensures that at least some income continues to come in during recovery.

Insurance will also help cover the costs to repair the car. If it's a two-car crash and the person in the other car is injured, your insurance will help pay medical costs for that person if you caused the accident.

This one scenario points out the importance of insurance. Insurance would cover your hospital and doctor bills; medical costs for people injured in the other car; repair of your own car, and income while you recover from any injuries. Without insurance, your costs could easily exceed $100,000. You could then be in debt for several years and may even need to consider filing for bankruptcy.

Insurance You Need

Let's look at the most important kinds of insurance that you need, along with a description of each.

Health

This covers medical, dental, and vision. Most employers offer all three. If you are one of the millions of Americans who have part-time or seasonal employment; you will need to find an insurance broker that can provide you with an insurance plan that covers catastrophic injuries or illnesses. Though the broker may not be able to find a plan that is affordable, I have used a broker to find reasonable healthcare for my daughter that is less expensive than my employer's plan. I also recommend *www.healthcare.gov* to search for competitive rates.

Auto

This protects your car against damage or loss. Most policies also cover bodily injury sustained by you, any passengers, and other drivers. There are three categories of auto insurance: liability, comprehensive, and collision.

Homeowners, Condominium, and Renters

This protects against damage to your home. You may also insure valuables inside the home, such as furniture, jewelry, and electronics, in case of theft. This is one area where many young people who rent try to save money. My advice: don't skip this insurance.

Even if you are the best tenant possible; another person in the apartment complex could make a bad choice and the consequences can affect everyone. For example, assume that you have just purchased a new laptop, smart phone, iPad, and $500 worth of new jeans. You have been saving for two years to get these items. Next door, your neighbor is having a huge party. At 2 a.m., someone with too much to drink falls asleep on the sofa with a cigarette in his or her hand. A fire breaks out and everyone escapes with just the clothes on their backs. You can't salvage anything. Unless you purchased extended warranties for your new items, they are gone and two years of saving has gone down the drain.

Disability

This pays a specific amount, or a percentage of your income, if you cannot work due to a disability. Many employers offer this type of insurance as a benefit and some pay for it with no cost to the employee. If you are a single-income household, it is critical that you have some type of disability insurance to cover lost income should you experience an injury.

Life

Life insurance provides income for family members upon your death. There are three general categories for life insurance:

1. Term: covers a specific period of time, usually offers lower premiums, and does not build a cash value.

2. Whole Life: offers a cash buildup option and premiums that do not increase over time.

3. Universal: provides flexible terms that allow for adjustments to the policy as your situation changes.

Long-Term Care

This is health insurance, usually for older Americans, which covers those with a chronic illness or disability that leaves you unable to care for yourself over an extended period.

Insurance Provided to Military Veterans

You need to be aware of two kinds of insurance available for veterans.

Life Insurance

As a service member, your life was insured for the maximum of $400,000. The Veterans Affairs Department administers the Servicemembers' Group Life Insurance (SGLI) program and the Veterans' Group Life Insurance (VGLI) program.

When you leave the military, the SGLI insurance policy does not go with you. However, you can transfer it into the VGLI. This insurance will cost more, but it is available automatically and no physical exam is required. However, your coverage must be converted into the VGLI program within 120 days of separation.

Coverage is available, regardless of medical condition, such as illness or war wounds. But shop around. Just make sure that you sign up for VGLI within the window. If you don't apply within the 120-day window, you may still have an opportunity to do so up to one year after leaving the service by following additional guidelines. To learn more, visit *www.insurance.va.gov* to submit an application.

Long-Term Care Insurance

This insurance helps protect people as they age and cannot care for themselves any longer. The Federal Long-Term Care Insurance Program is open to active duty and retired service members. You can learn more at *www.ltcfeds.com* or by calling 800-582-3337.

Although life and long-term care insurance are available to veterans through these programs, this means that you must shop around for every other kind of insurance policy. And if you didn't join the VGLI program after leaving military service, you'll also need to buy life insurance. The good news is that there are plenty of companies offering auto, life, homeowner's, and renter's insurance. Many life and disability policies can be obtained through your employer as well. Be sure to investigate your benefits package when you conduct your price comparison.

Automobile Insurance

All states require any licensed driver to be insured. However, most states only require liability insurance. You need to know all of the coverages available in a car insurance policy, so let's go through them.

Liability Insurance

If you are in a car accident, you are liable for the damage to the vehicle that has been hit, as well as any injuries to the driver and passengers in the other car.

This insurance is broken into three categories: the amount of money that the insurance company will pay for injuries to each person; the amount for all injuries per accident; and the amount of property damage. Three numbers will show you the amount of insurance for each category. One of the most common liability insurance policies provides the driver with 25/50/25 coverage limits. This means that the insurance policy will pay up to $25,000 to treat any injuries for each person in the accident; up to $50,000 for all injuries; and no more than $25,000 to cover property damage to the other car for each accident.

Personal Injury Protection (PIP)

This pays the expenses for any of your injuries, such as medical and hospital bills, not covered by your medical insurance. It can include protection against lost income if the accident causes you to miss work, as well as child care and funeral expenses.

Uninsured Motorist (UM) and Underinsured Motorist (UIM)

This protects you if the other driver is at fault and doesn't have car insurance. This insurance will help cover the costs of injuries, other medical costs, and repairing damage to your car. If the other driver doesn't have enough insurance, underinsured motorist coverage will plug the difference between your bills and the driver's coverage up to the limits of your policy.

Uninsured Motorist Property Damage (UMPD)

This will cover damage to your vehicle if the other driver is not insured.

Collision

Collision insurance will pick up the costs if your car is damaged in an accident. Liability covers the cost of repairs for someone else's property. And comprehensive insurance covers a variety of events, such as theft or a flying rock hitting your windshield.

Understand that collision insurance usually covers the retail value of your car, not the amount owed to pay off the car. Therefore, you may also want to consider "gap" insurance, which picks up the difference if you owe more on your car than it is actually worth. If your car is paid off and is older, you may want to lower your collision coverage because the retail value may be low.

Comprehensive

This coverage protects against theft, vandalism, fire, and other circumstances not related to a collision.

Roadside Assistance and Other Extras

This covers a wide variety of services, from towing to the cost of a rental car. I seriously recommend purchasing some of these services. For example, if your car has severe damage and will take several days to repair, the weekly cost of a rental car can be $150 or more.

The Cost of Insurance

The price you pay for car insurance depends on a wide variety of factors. These include the following:

★ The cost and age of your car. This one's pretty much a no-brainer: an expensive, newer model car will cost more to insure than a five-year-old sedan.

★ The age and gender of the drivers. It costs more to insure men than women, though rates begin to ease for people age 25 and older.

★ The amount of the deductible for collision insurance. Deductibles typically run between $0 and $1,000. A policy with a deductible of $1,000 will cost less, but you will be responsible for paying $1,000 if your car is damaged in any accident.

★ Your driving record, which includes speeding tickets, accidents, and claim history play a large role.

★ Insurance companies will also factor in where you live and how much you drive.

★ A good credit history will work in your favor.

★ Finally, each state will specify a required limit of liability coverage. And if you owe money on your auto loan or have a lease, your lender or lease holder may require collision and comprehensive coverage.

Shopping for Auto Insurance

Armed with this information, the good news is that shopping for car insurance can be done from the privacy of your home. Visit the Websites of various insurance companies, plug in all of the information required and compare rates. Also, make certain to look for discounts that can lower your monthly premium. Most companies offer discounts for insuring more than one vehicle, buying other types of insurance with them, such as homeowner's insurance, and a safe driving record.

A second strategy is to speak directly with representatives of some of the largest insurers, then contact an independent agent who can quote premiums from a variety of companies. Once you compare coverages and costs, you'll have a complete picture of your insurance needs.

A third strategy is to use your network of friends and other veterans to find a representative who you can trust and consult for many years. Think about it: you will need auto and other insurance coverage for most of your life, so finding an expert (especially if he or she is a veteran) who can save you money and provide peace of mind over the long haul can be a good long-term decision.

Whatever policy and coverage you choose, keep in mind that the more expensive your vehicle, the more assets you own, and the higher your income, the more insurance you will need.

Mechel's Tips on Car Insurance

Based on my personal experience of purchasing car insurance for approximately 20 years, here's what I would add:

★ If you are a safe driver—and that means rarely causing an accident or receiving a speeding ticket—opt for a deductible of at least $500, and possibly higher. A higher deductible will lower your monthly payment. But it also means that you will pay more out-of-pocket costs if you do get into an accident.

★ If your car is 7–10 years old, you probably don't need to buy collision or comprehensive insurance. If your 10-year-old car is severely damaged in an accident, but the car is only worth a couple of thousand dollars, you probably want to get a new car.

★ Many sales positions require a clean driving record. If you want a career in sales, make certain to drive safely and do not incur any speeding tickets.

★ Take a defensive driving class. These are now offered online and help refresh your memory on constantly changing traffic laws. They could also help to lower your insurance premiums.

Homeowner's Insurance

As with car insurance, homeowner's insurance policies vary by insurance company, state law, and the type of home. Here are some of the basic standard policies you might run across.

Just about every homeowner needs to insure his or her home for the amount it would cost to rebuild it, not its market value. If your home burns to the ground, the insurer will reimburse you for rebuilding the house. Construction costs might be more or less than the home's market value. Remember, the cost to rebuild should not include the value of the land.

Too many people find out the hard way that they underinsured their homes. After disaster strikes, they learn the home insurance money isn't enough to rebuild the house. United Policyholders, a consumer-advocacy group in San Francisco, offers a wealth of information about how to make sure you have enough insurance, including tips from disaster survivors.

The coverage for contents—furniture, clothing, and other belongings—is typically a portion, such as 50 percent, of the home's insured value. If your dwelling is insured for $300,000, for instance, the contents coverage would be $150,000.

You can get more coverage for belongings by paying a higher premium. To find out how much insurance you need for contents, do a thorough inventory. The Insurance Information Institute provides free home-inventory software at KnowYourStuff.org. Besides helping you determine how much coverage to buy, a thorough inventory will also help you work with the insurance company if you ever need to make a claim.

Keep in mind that home insurance policies typically cap the amount of coverage for valuables, such as fine art, jewelry, coins, antiques, and other precious items. You'll need to buy extra coverage for those items.

Understand the difference between actual cash value and replacement cost coverage. Actual cash value coverage reimburses you for the cost of the lost or damaged item minus depreciation. So if fire destroys your 10-year-old TV, you're reimbursed for the value of a 10-year-old TV. Replacement cost coverage reimburses you for the cost to buy a new TV.

Replacement cost coverage is pricier than actual cash value coverage, but you'll be glad to have it if you ever lose everything in a disaster.

How Home Insurance Is Priced

Home insurance premiums vary according to the amount and type of coverage you buy, where you live, the insurer offering the coverage, the deductible, and your credit and loss history. Insure.com has published tips on 15 ways to save on home insurance.

Understand, though, that home insurance doesn't protect your home against everything. You need to buy separate flood insurance and earthquake insurance policies to cover damage from those perils. For more, see what your policy won't cover at *www.insure.com*.

Finally, home insurance isn't something you buy once and forget about until you sell the house. Insurance agents recommend reviewing your coverage once a year to make sure you have sufficient coverage. You should increase coverage whenever you remodel or improve the home.

Renter's Insurance

Just like a homeowner's policy, if you are a renter, you can purchase renter's insurance which is a policy that provides actual cash value or replacement cost coverage for your belongings. Replacement cost coverage will cost you more in premiums, but it will also pay out more if you ever need to file a claim.

Always tell your agent about the valuable items you own. Jewelry, antiques, and electronics might be covered only up to an amount that won't pay for their replacement. Also, people who work out of their homes should consider policies that provide the full replacement cost of any items that could be damaged or stolen.

If you have some items that are unusually expensive, such as a diamond ring, you'll probably want to purchase a separate rider. Without riders for expensive items, you can't recover the full loss if it's beyond your policy limit.

Mechel's Tips on Homeowner's and Renter's Insurance

Homeowners and renters with expensive equipment or valuables have the greatest need for insurance.

One of the best deterrents to a thief is an electronic home security system, so consider having one installed. Although the installation cost can run several hundred dollars, monthly maintenance fees are usually under $20. You could obtain a discount on your insurance premiums by having an actively monitored system installed.

To protect and document the types of valuables you have, you should write down the serial numbers of those items and take pictures of the valuables in your home.

Additionally, most people have a video feature on their smart phone. A 60-second video walking through your house is a good way to show the valuables you want protected in the event of loss.

Finally, for people who need both car and homeowner's insurance, many companies offer a discount if you decide to buy both policies with the same company. As car and homeowner's insurance will cost thousands of dollars a year, you may be able to cut hundreds of dollars of the combined cost of these two policies.

Filing an Insurance Claim

If you are involved in a car accident or your home is burglarized, you'll file a claim with your insurance companies to receive money to cover damages and other costs. Here are steps you will need to take.

Contact your insurance company immediately. By informing them of the details of the accident and your intent to file a claim, they'll provide the forms and other information needed to file a claim.

Provide documents and other details. If a claim involves another party, get their insurance information. Also get the names of any witnesses and file a report with the local police department. If you are on the scene of a car accident or arrive home shortly after any damage or theft, take photos to submit as part of the claim.

Plan for deductibles and related expenses. Know the amount of your deductible and be prepared to pay for required out-of-pocket expenses. In some cases, your insurance provider may require you to submit proof of payment and reimburse you.

Compare deductibles and projected payouts. Compare the out-of-pocket deductible amount with the estimated insurance payout and choose the best option. In some cases, too many small claims could result in higher insurance rates or changes to future coverage.

Research alternative options. If a tornado or other natural disaster causes damage to your home and property, federal or state disaster relief assistance may be available. For more information, visit *www.disasterassistance.com* and *www.fema.gov*.

Retain documents. Keep a record of all expenses and documents related to any accident or event. This information includes a list of damaged or lost assets, receipts from car rentals, hotel stays, and hospital visits.

What to Expect When Filing an Insurance Claim

After you have filed a claim, your insurance company will review it and notify you of the amount the insurance will pay.

If you believe that your initial claim was denied for the wrong reasons, talk to your insurance company. If you believe that your policy covers the damage, submit the claim again.

Once a claim has been approved, the insurance company may reimburse you for medical bills, victim or beneficiary expenses, or repairs. Stay in touch with the insurance provider regarding adjuster appointments, any documents needed, and estimated payouts.

Insurance Checklist

Use this chart to help identify your insurance needs. In the left column, check the insurance coverage you have currently. Then, in the right column, check the coverage you have an interest in.

✓	**Insurance I Have**	✓	**Insurance I Need**
	Health		Health
	Dental		Dental
	Vision		Vision
	Critical Illness		Critical Illness
	Term Life		Term Life
	Medigap		Medigap
	Whole Life		Whole Life
	Universal Life		Universal Life
	Long-Term Care		Long-Term Care
	Homeowners'		Homeowners'
	Renters'		Renters'

	Auto		Auto
	Travel		Travel
	Disability		Disability
	Pet		Pet
	Umbrella		Umbrella
	Extended Warranties		Extended Warranties

Conclusion

As I've referenced many times throughout this book, when I was discharged from the U.S. Army more than 20 years ago, my financial life was in disarray. But, piece by piece, I built my own plan and began to execute it. I earned my college degree, began my career at one of the largest companies in the world, and eventually started my own company.

I bought my own home and have paid down a large chunk of my mortgage. I've established a savings plan for my daughter's college education while also putting aside money for my own retirement. Two decades after leaving military service, I'm in position to begin considering some long-term investments, such as a vacation home.

The purpose of this book is to help you build your own personal financial action plan. If you are facing some financial obstacles right now, the worksheets at the end of each chapter will help you understand how to attack specific financial problems and develop solutions. Whereas the book will provide a complete understanding about how to build your own plan, you can also attack individual issues. Whenever you have a financial problem or want to take action to fulfill a new goal, refer to the specific chapter and use the worksheets to get started.

I've made many specific recommendations about how you can build your plan by creating a budget, paying down debt, establishing long-term spending and savings habits, and protecting your assets, such as your home. However, I have not made specific recommendations about some financial products, such as insurance and investments. Although I do my own research and make my own investments, I do not have specific training or education in insurance or investments. I encourage you to do your own research to find the right experts in these areas.

In conclusion, I've experienced setbacks in my quest to conquer my finances. Like every other military service member, when I'm knocked down, I get up and fight back.

But I've also learned not to fight back alone. There is a team of people supporting you in the Armed Forces, and the same is true as a veteran. I strongly encourage you to seek assistance from the numerous resources and organizations I've provided in this book, especially if you are having trouble accessing the benefits you have earned. Finally, remember that if you have a plan and make a commitment to fulfill it, you can overcome any obstacle to the financial grenades life throws in your path. Good luck.

Index

About the Authors

Mechel Lashawn Glass is Vice President of Education for ClearPoint Credit Counseling Solutions, a national nonprofit financial counseling agency, and is responsible for all of the organization's financial education and literacy programs. Glass served in the United States Army from 1988 to 1992. After earning her bachelor's degree in international affairs, she worked as a certified project management professional and educator for IBM Corporation and started her own company called Beat Debt, Inc. She writes a monthly blog about personal finance for Equifax, one of the nation's largest credit bureaus. She lives in Atlanta, Georgia.

Scott Scredon owns his own public relations agency. He previously worked as the Director of Public Relations for a nonprofit credit counseling agency and for 19 years as a senior vice president for corporate communications for Bank of America Corporation. He also worked for five years as a bureau chief and correspondent for *BusinessWeek* magazine. He lives in metro Atlanta.